DATE DUE			

WHEELS
AT
WORK

Other Boston Children's Museum Activity Books by Bernie Zubrowski:

Ball-Point Pens

Bubbles

Messing Around with Baking Chemistry

Messing Around with Drinking Straws

Messing Around with Water Pumps

Milk Carton Blocks

Raceways: Having Fun with Balls and Tracks

WHEELS AT WORK

BUILDING AND EXPERIMENTING WITH MODELS
OF MACHINES

BERNIE ZUBROWSKI

ILLUSTRATED BY

ROY DOTY

A BOSTON CHILDREN'S MUSEUM ACTIVITY BOOK
WILLIAM MORROW AND COMPANY, INC./NEW YORK

Special thanks to Diane Willow and Angela Kimberk, who helped design and try out the models shown in this book. Thanks also to Gary Goldstein, who checked the accuracy of the scientific explanations. And extra special thanks to Patty Quinn, who helped me put the final manuscript into a clear and coherent form.

Library of Congress Cataloging-in-Publication Data

Zubrowski, Bernie.
Wheels at work.

Summary: Instructions for using readily available
materials to make models of machines such as pulleys,
windlasses, and water wheels, with suggested experiments to determine their capabilities.
1. Machinery—Models—Juvenile literature. 2. Wheels
—Juvenile literature. [1. Machinery—Models.
2. Machinery—Experiments. 3. Models and model making.
4. Handicraft. 5. Experiments] I. Doty, Roy,
1922- ill. II. Title.
TJ147.Z89 1986 621.8 86-12500
ISBN 0-688-06348-9 (lib. bdg.)
ISBN 0-688-06349-7 (pbk.)

To Evelyn

CONTENTS

WHEELS AT WORK

INTRODUCTION

Look around and try to imagine what the world would be like without wheels. Cars and buses and trains would all disappear, along with your bicycle, roller skates, or skateboard. Without pulleys to help lift heavy steel and stone, there would be no cities full of skyscrapers. Lights and power supplied by electricity from turbines would be shut off permanently. You would even have to learn to tell time by the sun because there would be no more gears inside clocks and watches. Can you think of more ways your life would change without the visible and invisible wheels we take for granted every day?

For thousands of years the wheel has been used to make people's work easier. We think the wheel was invented in an area of the world that is now the country of Syria in southwestern Asia. The first wheels were solid pieces of wood joined together to form circles, and eventually they became the familiar spoked wheels we see today.

The wheel is most frequently used on vehicles to allow them to move quickly and smoothly, but it can also be incorporated into other machines and devices to lift heavy weights or obtain power from moving air and water. This book describes some of the most important wheel devices that have enabled people to do different kinds of work that would have been very difficult if not impossible without them. You can follow the instructions to construct working models of these inventions. They're not only fun to build, but fascinating to watch in action. As you play and experiment with your models, you will learn how they work and begin to understand some basic ideas about how similar machines operate.

The materials for making these models are usually found around your house or can be obtained from a nearby hardware store. Although the techniques for construction have been kept as simple as possible, many of the models will present a great challenge. Sometimes you may have to try and fail and try again to get a model working just right. Inventors have to do lots of what they call trouble-shooting before they get their machines working right. After building several models and trouble-shooting them, you will have the experience of becoming an inventor yourself.

THE PULLEY

Imagine trying to lift a heavy piano from the first floor to the
second floor of a building. What would it be like trying to
carry the piano up a stairway? But if you hang a set of
pulleys off the roof and attach them to the piano, it could be
lifted into the air and passed through a window.

The useful pulley is one of the earliest and simplest wheel devices. No one knows when it was invented, but a picture from what is now Syria shows one in use back in the eighth century B.C.

It was discovered that a small wheel within a frame made it easier to pull up a heavy weight hanging from a rope running over the wheel. It was also learned that when more than one pulley was used, even less force was needed to lift heavy objects.

Engineers in ancient times used this knowledge to their advantage in the construction of many monuments and temples. The blocks of very heavy stone used in these buildings were moved by cranes made from long wooden poles, ropes, and pulleys.

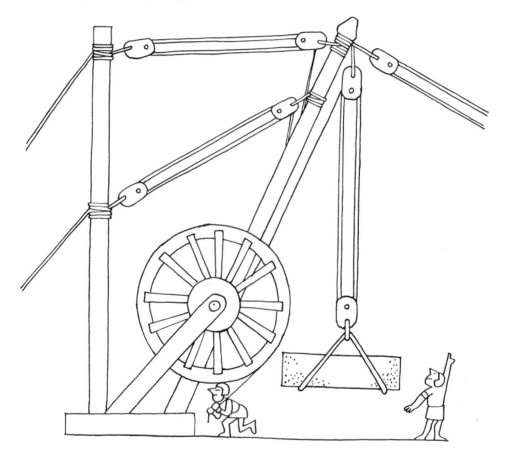

Pulleys are still very much in use today. You may see them around your neighborhood on a clothesline or on the flagpole outside your school. Mechanics in garages use a special pulley arrangement called a *differential* to lift engines out of cars. Similar kinds of pulleys are also used in factories to move heavy machinery.

MAKING A PULLEY ARRANGEMENT

To find out what pulleys can do, you should set them up in different arrangements. To do this you will need to have more than one on hand. Many hardware and department stores sell pulleys, and they are generally inexpensive. Since it is more fun and much more interesting to experiment with heavy weights, don't buy small toy pulleys.

Also get the type of pulley called a *clothesline spreader*. This has two wheels on the same frame. (When you are shopping for your pulleys, you may need to pick up a package of the right size rope, too.)

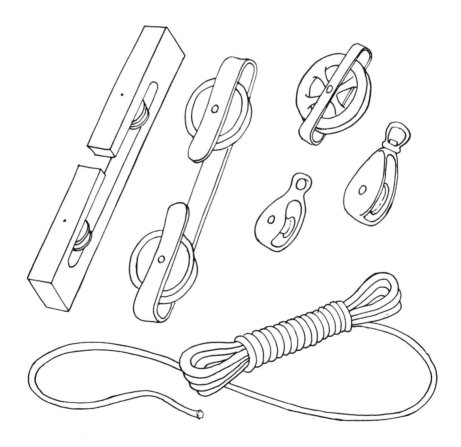

Making Weights

In order to experiment with different pulley arrangements, you will need weights. You can use almost any heavy objects you have around the house. Plastic containers with handles that have been filled with sand or water work well.

Paper milk cartons are also good to use, and they will give you uniform weights.

You will need:

> 3 or more empty paper half-gallon milk cartons
> enough sand to fill the milk cartons
> 3 or more pieces of coat-hanger wire or any sturdy wire
> masking tape or stapler and staples

Step 1. Fill the empty milk cartons with sand.

Step 2. Tape or staple the tops closed securely to prevent any spillage.

Step 3. Push a coat-hanger wire through the top of each carton to serve as a handle. Bend the wire as shown.

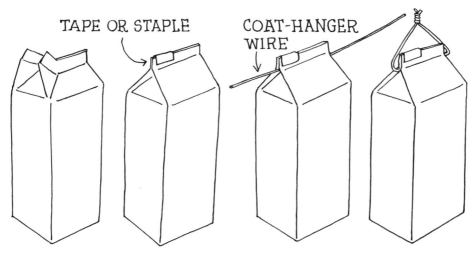

TAPE OR STAPLE   COAT-HANGER WIRE

SAFETY NOTE: Wear gloves when lifting a weight with pulleys. Sometimes the rope or pulley may slip. If you try to hold on to a fast-moving rope, it may burn your hands as it slides through.

SETTING UP

Before you can begin experimenting, you will have to hunt around your house for a suitable place to hang the pulleys. You could suspend them from a board placed between 2 tables, the backs of 2 chairs, or across the rungs of an open ladder.

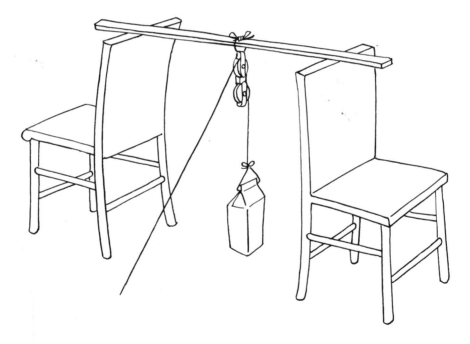

If you have ceiling beams (not pipes) somewhere in your home or classroom, you can tie the pulleys to one of them. Outside you could suspend the pulleys from a low-hanging tree branch.

EXPERIMENTS TO TRY

Once you've made some milk-carton weights and found a safe place to hang your pulleys, you're ready to experiment. Set up your pulley and weight as shown in each drawing. The route the rope takes as it goes around the wheels may get confusing, so study the drawings carefully before trying them yourself.

• There are two ways of using a single pulley to lift an object.

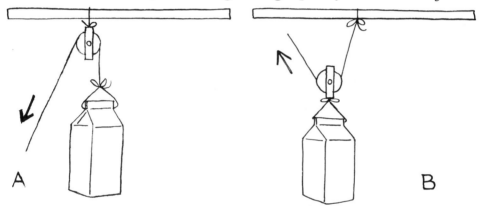

Which arrangement makes it easier to lift the milk-carton weight?

• Two pulleys can also be set up in two different ways.

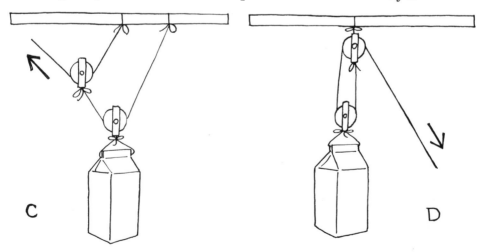

Does a two-pulley arrangement make it even easier to lift the milk-carton weight? Does the amount of force needed to lift the weight seem any different in either of the arrangements?

- Using two clothesline spreaders, try threading the rope through all four wheels, as shown.

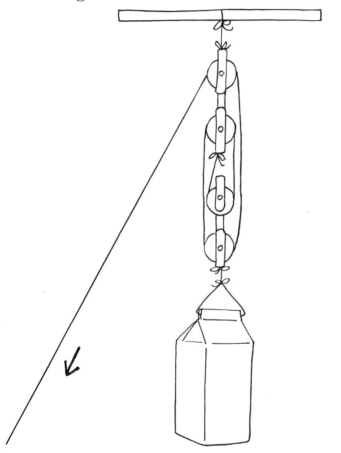

E

Does this arrangement make it easier to lift the same weight? How many milk cartons can you lift with this setup?

- Experiment with other ways of threading the rope through the pulley. Try adding more pulleys and rope to see if you can lift even heavier weights.

WHAT'S HAPPENING?

By now, you've found that the more pulleys you use, the easier it is to lift weights. You have also discovered that the way in which the rope is placed on the pulleys makes a difference. Pulleys may look simple, but careful thinking is required to understand how they operate.

You can begin to understand what is happening by starting with the idea of force. This word has several meanings, but here *force* means something special. Pushing or pulling on an object such as a weight is exerting a force on that object. When you pull on a standing wagon or lift a heavy suitcase, you are using the force of your body to make them move. Likewise, a milk-carton weight hanging by a piece of rope from a board is said to be exerting a force on the board. At the same time the board pulls up on the string with a force equal to the weight of the carton. If the board were not strong enough to do this, it would break and the weight would fall.

Of the two arrangements using a single pulley, the one with the rope attached to the board, arrangement B, requires less force. You can think of the board as helping you lift the weight. Half the weight is supported by you and half by the board.

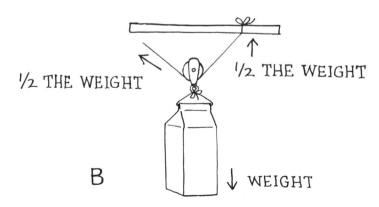

½ THE WEIGHT

½ THE WEIGHT

B

↓ WEIGHT

In arrangement A, the force needed to lift the weight is coming from your pulling on the rope. The wheel acts like a seesaw where a force on one end has to be equal to the weight of the object sitting on the other end. In this arrangement, the board has to support both the object and the force you are using to lift the object.

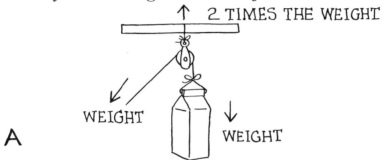

↑ 2 TIMES THE WEIGHT

WEIGHT   ↓ WEIGHT

A

When two pulleys were used, you should have discovered that arrangement C makes it easier to lift the milk-carton weight than D. You can understand why this happens by thinking of arrangement D as a combination of A and B. Instead of the second pulley hanging from the board as in B, it is now hanging from a pulley. But *this* pulley is connected directly to the board, so the weight of the milk carton is still shared by the board and you. The top pulley just allows you to change the direction of the rope and pull down instead of up, which is more comfortable for your muscles.

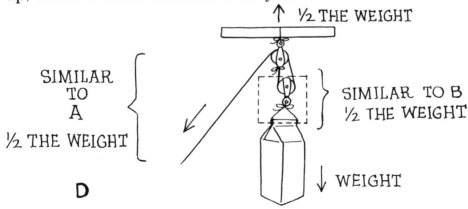

↑ ½ THE WEIGHT

SIMILAR
TO
A
½ THE WEIGHT

SIMILAR TO B
½ THE WEIGHT

↓ WEIGHT

D

Therefore, arrangement D requires less force than A, the same amount of force as B, and is more convenient than B.

Arrangement C requires even less force than D, however, because C doubles the action of B. In arrangement C the sections of rope on either side of the lower pulley each carry half the weight of the milk carton. But one of these ropes is now attached to a second pulley. The rope from the second pulley is in turn sharing half the load from the lower pulley between the board and you. So each section of this rope is sharing one half of one half the weight of the milk carton, or one fourth of the total weight. Your share of the weight has been reduced by a factor of four.

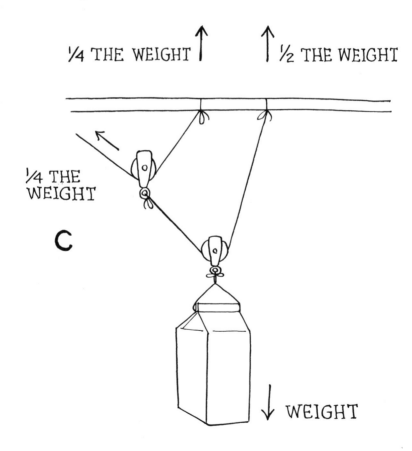

¼ THE WEIGHT   ½ THE WEIGHT

¼ THE
WEIGHT

C

↓ WEIGHT

Arrangement E can be broken down in the same way. The rope inside the boxed section is similar to arrangement D, which we know reduces by half the force required to lift the milk-carton weight. But this rope continues on and goes around another lower pulley, which is attached to the other pulley hanging from the board. This reduces by half again the force required to lift the weight. Combining the two sets of pulleys this way results in your share of the force needed to lift the weight being reduced to one fourth of the total weight of the object. Arrangement E is like using D twice.

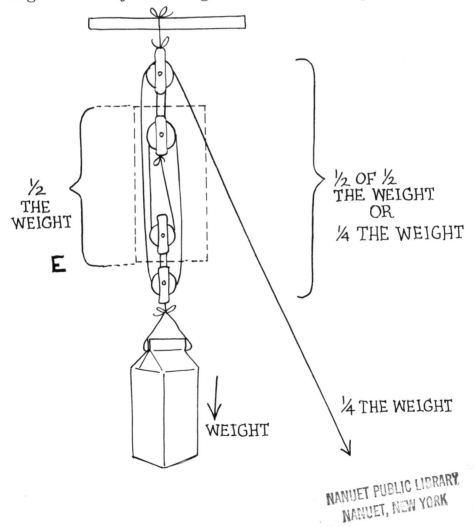

½ THE WEIGHT

E

½ OF ½ THE WEIGHT OR ¼ THE WEIGHT

WEIGHT

¼ THE WEIGHT

More pulleys could be combined and the result would be that even less force would be needed to lift the weight. However, as you saw when going from two to four pulleys, the more pulleys you use, the more rope you have to pull to lift the weight up to the board. The advantage of a pulley system is that it enables you to lift a very heavy weight using a small amount of force, but this force has to be exerted over a long time or distance to move the object more and more easily.

It may be hard to appreciate the advantages of using pulleys when lifting small weights, but remember the example of the piano.

The next time you are near an automobile repair shop, a boatyard, or a construction site, look around to find more examples of pulleys at work.

THE WINDLASS

If you have ever seen an old-fashioned wishing well, then you have seen a windlass.

This wheel-and-axle device is found on farms or next to old country houses, where it is used on top of water wells to lift buckets of water.

The windlass originated several thousand years ago with the Babylonians and is about as old as the pulley. You will remember that in the pulley arrangement the rope moved continuously around the wheel. In a windlass the rope is wound up onto the cylinder-shaped wheel itself.

In ancient and medieval times the windlass was often used to haul up ore from mines or to open and close the very heavy gates of water canals. They were also used on boats to hoist sails and lift anchors. Today a similar device called a *capstan* is used on large ships to raise their very heavy anchors. The cable of the anchor is wound around a vertical post that is turned by bars at the top of this drum or is moved by the ship's engine.

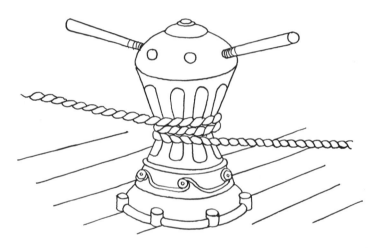

MAKING A WINDLASS

Find out for yourself how a windlass works by making a model of one. It only takes a few materials to construct, and it can be quickly assembled.

You will need:

  1 broomstick or large dowel, 3 feet long by 1 inch in diameter
  1 dowel or stick, 2 feet long by 1/4 inch in diameter
  2 one-pound coffee cans, with plastic lids
  2 nails, at least 2 inches long
  rope, 8 feet long

milk-carton weights with wire hooks attached (see
   page 18)
hammer
string or rubber bands
masking tape

Step 1. The plastic lid has a raised dot in its center. Place
the lid on the bottom of the can. Punch a small hole
with a nail through the lid and the bottom of the can.
   Enlarge this hole with a pointed stick so that the
broomstick can slide through.
   Do this for both coffee cans.

Step 2. Push the broomstick through the lids and cans.
Then tape the 2 cans together as shown in the
drawing.

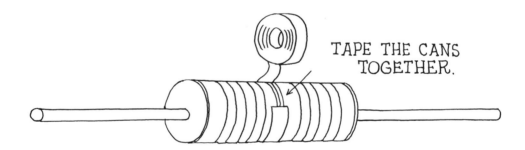

TAPE THE CANS
TOGETHER.

Step 3. Hammer the 2 nails through the sides of the cans
and into the broomstick.

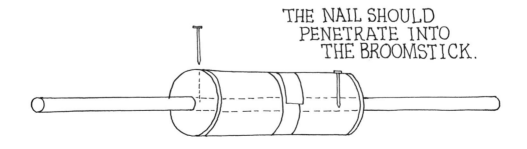

THE NAIL SHOULD
PENETRATE INTO
THE BROOMSTICK.

Step 4. Tie the smaller dowel or stick to one end of the broomstick. Then tie or tape one end of the rope to the cans.

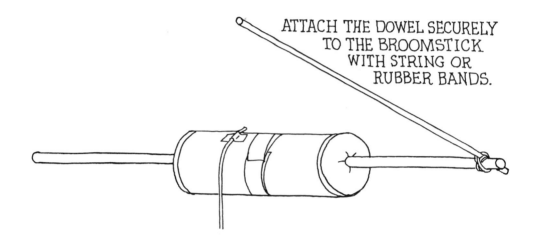

ATTACH THE DOWEL SECURELY TO THE BROOMSTICK WITH STRING OR RUBBER BANDS.

Step 5. Place your model between the tops of 2 chairs for support.

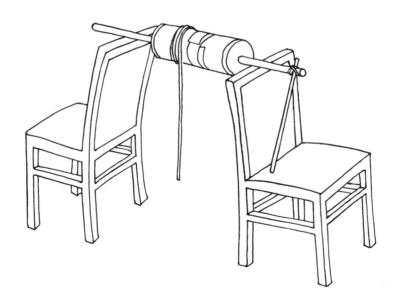

EXPERIMENTS TO TRY

- Attach a milk-carton weight to the free end of the rope. Turn the stick, or crank, to lift the weight up to the cans.

Start out lifting just one weight. Then add one more at a time. What happens to the force needed to turn the crank as more and more weights are added?

- Experiment with different ways of attaching or hanging the rope from the cans. Here are some examples.

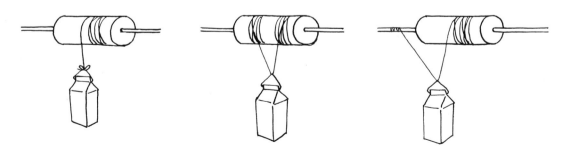

Does this affect the force needed?

- Try turning the crank while holding it farther and farther out on the stick. How does the amount of force needed change as you push farther away from the crank?
- Make another windlass using tin cans with a different diameter, or try using just the broomstick. Do these changes make a difference in the force needed to lift the weights?

WHAT'S HAPPENING?

When you construct a windlass, you are combining two simple machines—the wheel-and-axle, and the lever. Together these basic machines create a very effective device for lifting heavy weights.

The rope collects on the coffee-can drum, or wheel, which revolves on the broomstick, or axle. The force of the weight pulling on the rope is transferred from the wheel to the axle to the chair frame, which in turn rests on the ground. In this way the different parts of the windlass share the work of supporting the weight with you.

THE CHAIR FRAME HELPS SUPPORT THE WEIGHT.

In addition, the stick, or crank, used to rotate the coffee-can drum acts as a lever. You can understand what is happening by recalling your experiences with a seesaw. Think of the plank of a seesaw as the bar of a lever. The fixed support is the pivot point, or *fulcrum.* Force applied at one point along the plank, or lever, is used to lift or hold a person or weight placed at some other point.

To balance a friend who is the same weight as you, both of you must sit equal distances from the fulcrum.

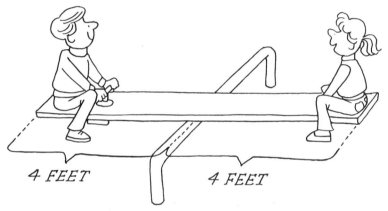

4 FEET   4 FEET

The only way for you to lift a heavy adult off the ground is to have the adult sit near the fulcrum. If an adult sits near the fulcrum, where should you sit?

4 FEET   1 FOOT

The operation of the seesaw shows how you can move a heavy object using a long bar. You should place the fulcrum near the object and apply a force far away from the object and fulcrum.

HERE A LARGE FORCE
IS NEEDED TO
MOVE THE ROCK.

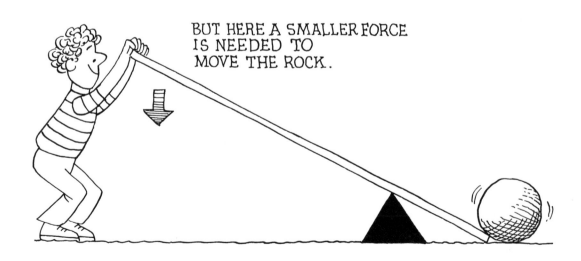

BUT HERE A SMALLER FORCE
IS NEEDED TO
MOVE THE ROCK.

The crank on the wheel-and-axle acts in a similar way. The farther out on the crank you apply your force, the easier it is to turn the drum. However, the farther out you go, the greater the distance you have to keep pushing to move the weight the same distance.

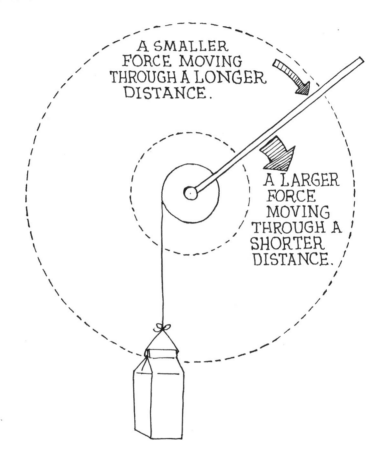

A SMALLER FORCE MOVING THROUGH A LONGER DISTANCE.

A LARGER FORCE MOVING THROUGH A SHORTER DISTANCE.

And you should have found that changing the diameter of the tin cans you use doesn't have much effect.

You may have observed that the pulley and the windlass have similar actions. In both devices the advantage of using less force to lift a weight must be compensated, or made up, for by applying that force over a greater distance.

THE GEAR

If you could look inside almost any kind of machinery that has moving parts, you would probably find some gears. These toothed wheels are an important part of mechanical clocks, automobile transmissions, and small appliances such as electric mixers.

Gears were invented in ancient times but were not used that much because they were difficult to make. The Egyptians and Greeks used them in water clocks and various kinds of mechanical devices that were more like toys than useful machines.

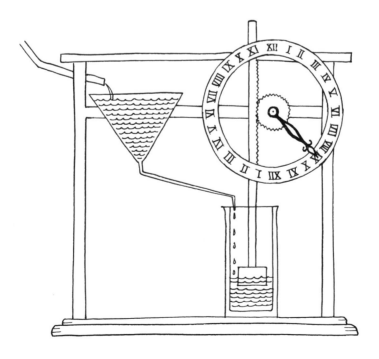

The Romans connected them to water wheels that helped turn the large stones that ground wheat into flour.

As the knowledge of working with metals grew and craftsmen became more skillful, the use of gears increased. For example, the first mechanical clocks had only a few very big gears. These clocks were so large they could be located only in places like church towers.

Over a period of two or three hundred years, gears were made smaller and smaller. More gears could fit wherever they were needed, and clocks and other devices gradually became the size we see them today.

A ten-speed bike is one of the few machines where you are able to see the action of the gears. To watch them operate, you can lift the rear wheel off the ground and give it a spin. You can get a feel for how gears work by riding the bike up a hill using the low gears and then shifting to the higher ones as you move downhill. You'll learn more about how and why gears work as you build your own set of model gears and do some experiments.

MAKING A SET OF GEARS

Making model gears is a real challenge because the teeth have to be very carefully aligned; that is, they have to be made to fit together just right. A set of gears can be put together using plastic cups for the teeth and cardboard for the wheel. This model will not be strong enough to lift heavy weights, but it can be used to find out how the speed of small gears changes when they are joined together in different combinations.

You will need:

> large pieces of cardboard from packing cartons for refrigerators or other appliances, or similar size boxes
>
> 9 tuna cans
>
> 8 plastic cups (3-ounce size)
>
> 40 plastic cups (7-ounce size)
>
> 3 pieces of coat-hanger wire or any sturdy wire, each 12 inches long
>
> 6 thick rubber bands
>
> 3 ball-point pen tubes
>
> yardstick
>
> 1-inch-wide masking tape
>
> mat knife
>
> hammer
>
> 1 nail
>
> pencil

Step **1.** To draw uniform circles for your wheels, you will first need to construct a circle maker. Hammer a nail through one end of the yardstick. Then make three more holes along the stick at distances of 3 inches, 8 inches, and 13 inches. (These holes should be just large enough for a pencil point to go through to the other side. Where they are placed determines the size of the circles you will make.)

NAIL

HOLES MADE WITH A NAIL BIG ENOUGH FOR A PENCIL POINT.

Step 2. Push the nail down into the cardboard to anchor the yardstick. Insert the pencil into one hole at a time and turn the yardstick in a circle. Draw and cut out:

2 circles, 3 inches in radius

2 circles, 8 inches in radius

2 circles, 13 inches in radius

Step 3. Place 1 tuna can in the center of the 6-inch wheel and tape it securely into place.

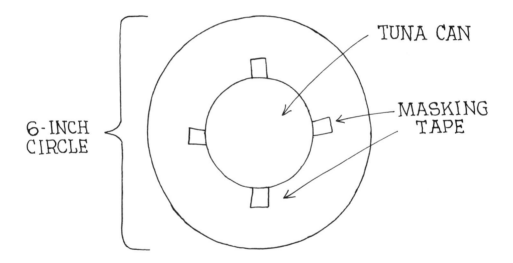

Punch a hole through the center of the cardboard wheel and can with the hammer and nail. Line up the other 6-inch circle on the other side of the tuna can. Punch a hole through the center of that wheel, too.

Step 4. Push a ball-point pen tube through the center of the circle, the can, and the other circle. Secure the tube in place by wrapping a thick rubber band around the tube next to each piece of cardboard.

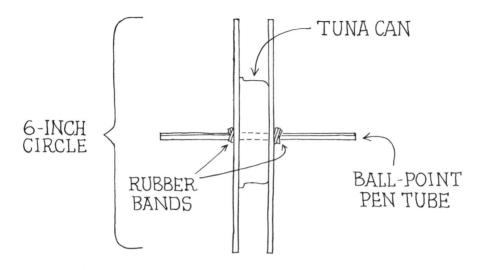

6-INCH CIRCLE

TUNA CAN

RUBBER BANDS

BALL-POINT PEN TUBE

Step 5. Punch a hole through the center of the two 16-inch circles. Place 4 tuna cans on one of the circles as shown in the drawing and tape them into place.

Line up the other 16-inch circle and push a ball-point pen tube through the center of both pieces of cardboard. Secure the tube with rubber bands.

Step 6. Repeat this procedure for the 26-inch circles.

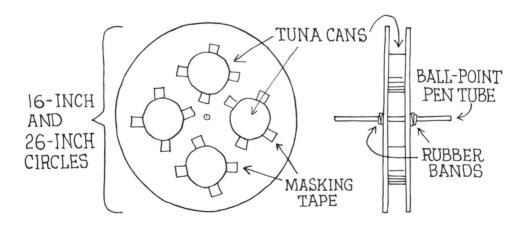

16-INCH AND 26-INCH CIRCLES

TUNA CANS

BALL-POINT PEN TUBE

MASKING TAPE

RUBBER BANDS

Step 7. To make the teeth of the smaller gear, join eight 3-ounce cups together with pieces of masking tape, as shown. Do not leave any gaps between the cups.

THE TAPE GOES ON THE INSIDE OF EACH CUP.

Step 8. Place the row of cups top side down around the edge of the two circles of the 6-inch wheel. Secure the cups to the wheel by placing strips of masking tape between the cups.

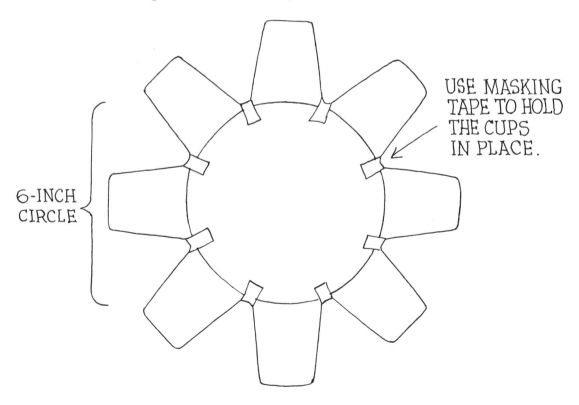

6-INCH CIRCLE

USE MASKING TAPE TO HOLD THE CUPS IN PLACE.

Step 9. For the middle size gear, repeat steps 7 and 8, using 16 seven-ounce cups.

Step 10. For the largest gear, repeat steps 7 and 8, using 24 seven-ounce cups. However, place them ¾ inch apart.

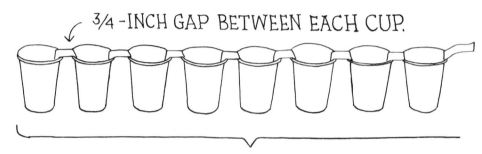

¾-INCH GAP BETWEEN EACH CUP.

CAREFULLY TAPE 24 CUPS TOGETHER KEEPING A ¾-INCH GAP.

Lay the wheel and the cups on the floor. Then tape the cups to the wheel. The spacing of each cup is very important, so take your time in taping them together and onto the wheel.

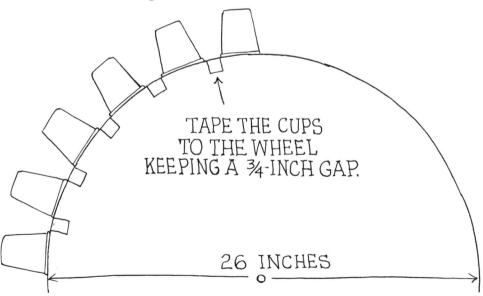

TAPE THE CUPS TO THE WHEEL KEEPING A ¾-INCH GAP.

26 INCHES

Step 11. Push a piece of coat-hanger wire through each ball-point pen tube. After you have carefully positioned the gears, tape the wires of the axles to the table so that they will remain in the same positions when operated.

GEARING UP

You will need to support your gears between two long tables or a group of chairs, to allow them to move freely. About an inch of the teeth of one gear should interlock with the teeth of another gear. If the gears are placed too close to each other, they might jam in certain spots because the alignment of the teeth is not exact. You can position them in any order.

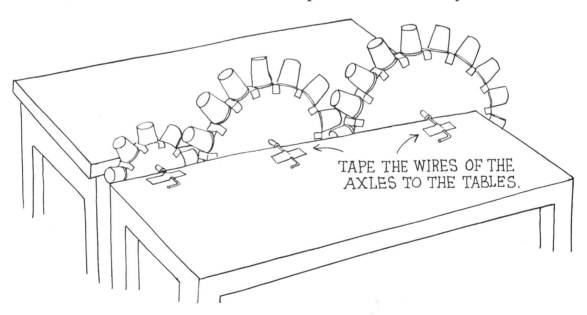

TAPE THE WIRES OF THE
AXLES TO THE TABLES.

To operate your model, push on one of the teeth from an outer wheel. When you have the gears working at slow speeds, try moving them faster.

EXPERIMENTS TO TRY

- Watch how the different-size gears move. Which one moves the fastest? Which one is slowest? Do any gears move at the same speed?
- Place the gears in different orders and see what changes, if any, this makes.
- If the gears are lined up in a row—small, medium, and large—how many turns does the small gear make when the large one is moved one revolution?
- How much does the large gear move when the smallest one is turned one revolution?
- Try lifting small weights by attaching one end of a string to the objects and the other end to a section of the cardboard. Is it easier to lift the weights when they are attached to the small gear or the big one?

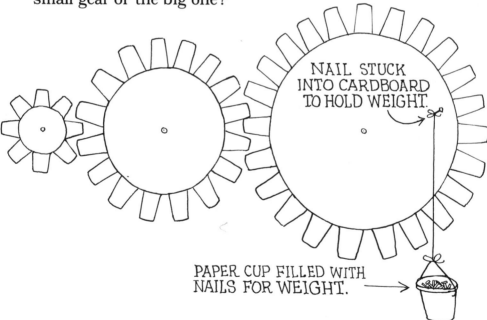

NAIL STUCK INTO CARDBOARD TO HOLD WEIGHT.

PAPER CUP FILLED WITH NAILS FOR WEIGHT. →

WHAT'S HAPPENING?

Gears provide a simple way of changing speed, or multiplying or reducing the power of a motor or machine. This is why they are used on bicycles and automobiles.

The action of changing speed was demonstrated by the three gears you made. Moving the big gear one revolution causes the smallest one to revolve three times. On the other hand, moving the smallest gear one revolution results in the big gear moving only one third of a revolution.

Gears are also used to increase or decrease the force needed to get a vehicle moving and keep it moving at certain rates. When it is first starting off, a vehicle needs enough power to overcome its own weight. Once it is moving, a smaller amount of power will allow it to keep up its momentum, or speed.

This effect can be seen and experienced when you are operating a ten-speed bike. The smaller size low gears are used to get you started or moving up a hill. They help you exert a lot of force on the rear wheel. The larger size higher gears are used when the bike is already moving. They allow you to supply a smaller force on the back wheel and still keep up the *momentum,* or forward movement, of the bike.

In order to understand this action better, it is helpful to imagine the gears acting as levers. Recall your experience with the windlass. The crank was attached to the broomstick axle on which there was a coffee-can cylinder with weights. The axle acts as a pivot point, or fulcrum, for the crank to act as a lever. Now imagine that the stick crank has been turned into a circle of cardboard. Turning the outer edge of this wheel also turns the coffee-can cylinder.

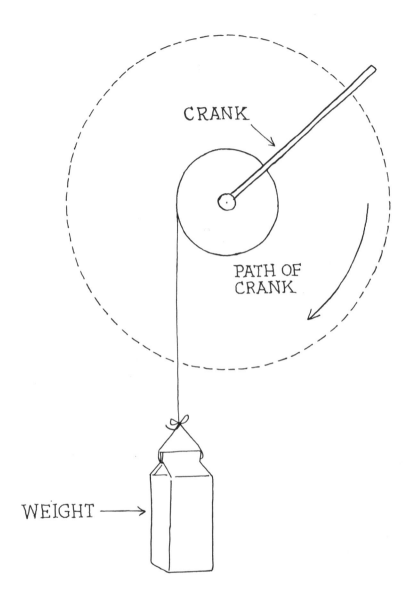

CRANK

PATH OF
CRANK

WEIGHT ⟶

The larger the wheel, the greater the force that can be applied to the coffee-can cylinder for a given force on the larger wheel. This is because, similar to the windlass and the seesaw, the greater the distance from the fulcrum at which the force is applied, the more force is exerted at the other end.

You can see this clearly if you put a small gear on the same axle as a big one and turn each of them. Less force is needed to turn the larger gear than the smaller one. And more force will result when the larger gear is turned.

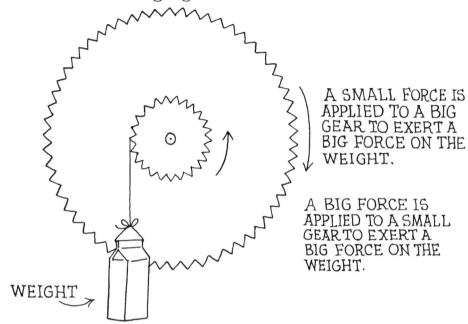

A SMALL FORCE IS APPLIED TO A BIG GEAR TO EXERT A BIG FORCE ON THE WEIGHT.

A BIG FORCE IS APPLIED TO A SMALL GEAR TO EXERT A BIG FORCE ON THE WEIGHT.

WEIGHT

Gears lined up in a series also can multiply a force. To understand how this happens, you must first understand what happens with a single gear. When a force is acting on one side of a gear, the same amount of force is felt on the other side.

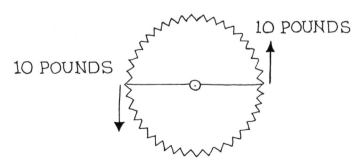

10 POUNDS

10 POUNDS

Gears of different sizes lined up in a series can also multiply a force. The same principles that apply to the seesaw, the windlass, and the other kinds of gear arrangement also are acting in this situation. Here it is helpful to think of the gear as a circular seesaw or balance. Weight placed on one end of the gear exerts a force equal to that weight on the opposite side of the *same* gear, but in the opposite direction. This means that the gear can be prevented from rotating only if a weight is placed at point B equal in magnitude to that at point A.

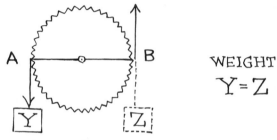

If you choose a larger diameter gear, the same action happens. However, placing the same amount of weight on the larger gear does result in a very important difference. Since this same amount of weight is now acting over a greater distance from the fulcrum, which is the center of the gear, the force exerted at point B for this larger gear is greater than that exerted at point B for the smaller gear.

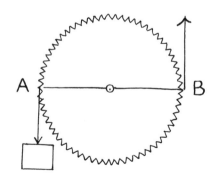

Keeping this in mind, consider what happens when gears of the same size are lined up in a series. If a weight hangs from point A, the force at point B is of the same magnitude. By having this arrangement, you change the direction of the force but not the magnitude.

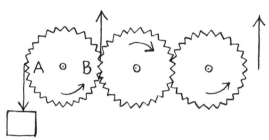

Now put a larger gear next to one of these gears and have the *same* weight on the *larger* gear. Since the gear is of a larger diameter, it is exerting a *larger* force at the opposite side. This means that the right-hand gear now is being made to rotate with a force greater than in the previous situation.

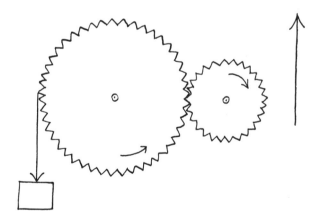

Going in the opposite direction, suppose the same weight is placed on the smaller of the two gears. Since this is a smaller diameter gear, this weight acts over a shorter distance. Its effect will be to rotate the larger gear, but not with the same force as the larger gear rotates the smaller one.

THE WATER WHEEL

Human and animal energy powered the early wheel devices you have been experimenting with so far. People continued to search, however, for a way to harness the natural forces of air and water.

The ancient Greeks invented a way to turn the wheel using the moving water of a river. Then, in the first century B.C., a Roman engineer named Vituvius designed the first practical water wheel. Buckets were placed on the rim of the wheel, and water falling into the buckets caused the wheel to turn. Another arrangement had wooden blades on the perimeter, which were pushed by the river.

The main use of these wheels was to turn the very heavy millstones that ground grain into flour. Whole grain was poured into a hole in the middle of the top stone. The grain was then crushed between the two flat round stones as they rotated, and pushed out the edge as flour. Gears were used to change the vertical motion of the water wheel into the horizontal motion of the grinding stones.

For several hundred years the water wheel was used only for grinding grain. Gradually it came to be used for powering all sorts of machinery. Water wheels made the blacksmith's work easier by tripping very heavy hammers and pumping huge bellows. Connected to saws, they provided the power to cut logs into timber. By the fourteenth and fifteenth centuries water wheels were used as a source of power in the manufacture of clothing, metals, and paper. In fact, the water wheel so often supplied the original force that set in motion the working parts of so many different machines that it became known as the "prime mover."

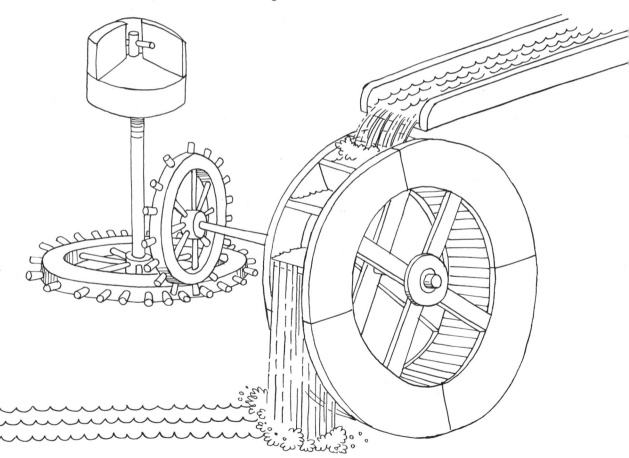

MAKING A VERTICAL WATER WHEEL

Experimenting with a model water wheel can be lots of fun.
You can make your wheel turn with water, and it will lift
weights and power even more complicated contraptions. You
don't have to build a model out of wood or metal. Ordinary
plastic cups and plates will do.

Since water will be poured on the model, plastic plates
work best. If you can't get plastic, use three or four heavy
paper plates taped together around the edges instead.

You will need:

> 4 plastic plates, 8 or 9 inches in diameter
> 24 plastic cups (3-ounce size)
> 1 ball-point pen tube
> 4 Styrofoam thread spools (1¼-inch size)
> masking tape, 1½ inches wide
> string, approximately 20 feet
> 1 nail
> scissors

Step 1. Punch a hole about ¼ inch in diameter through the
center of each plate. To find the center of cans or
plastic plates, find the point on the can or plate
where it balances on the eraser head of a pencil.

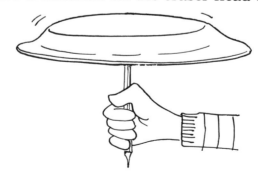

Step 2. Place 2 plates back to back and push the ball-point pen tube through the holes. Push the Styrofoam spools onto the pen tube against the outside of each plate. Repeat with the other 2 plates.

Step 3. Tape each set of plates together around the inside. (It would be helpful if someone held the plates while you taped them.)

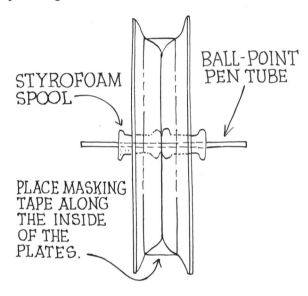

STYROFOAM SPOOL

BALL-POINT PEN TUBE

PLACE MASKING TAPE ALONG THE INSIDE OF THE PLATES.

Step 4. Cut 12 plastic cups in half as shown. (Save the part with the rim.)

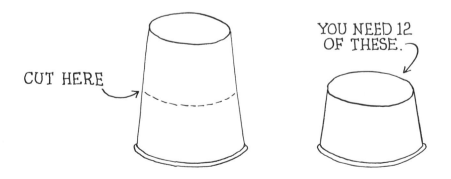

CUT HERE

YOU NEED 12 OF THESE.

Step 5. Tear off a strip of masking tape 25 inches long. Stick a whole cup to the masking tape sideways. Then slip the tape through the upper part of the cut cup. Slide this cup along the tape until it reaches and covers the whole cup. This arrangement will hold the whole cup securely in place.

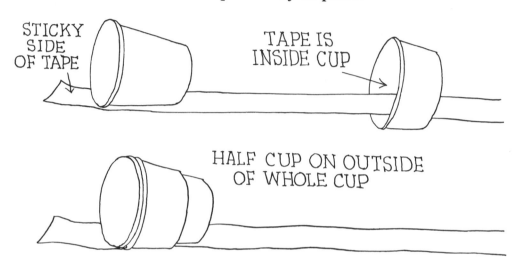

Step 6. Do this for the other 11 cups, positioning them ½ inch from each other.

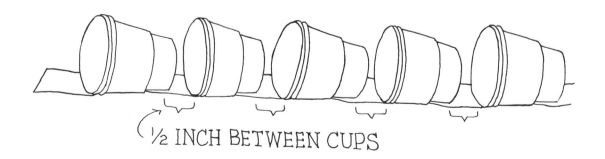

Step 7. Wrap this strip of cups around the edge of the second set of plates and secure it by taping each cup in place.

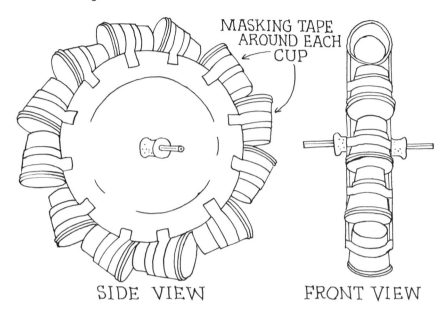

MASKING TAPE
AROUND EACH
← CUP

SIDE VIEW   FRONT VIEW

Step 8. Push the completed cup wheel and the other wheel until they are side by side on the pen tube. Tape these two wheels so that they will move together.

Step 9. Wrap about 20 feet of string around the empty wheel. This wheel will be the string collector.

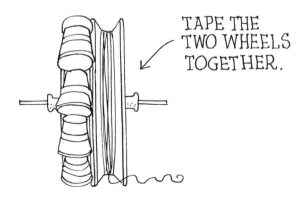

TAPE THE
TWO WHEELS
TOGETHER.

SETTING UP

The water wheel device should be positioned above a tray. If you make a stand for your model, it will be easier to do the experiments. (This stand will also be useful with several other wheel devices.)

You will need:

> 1 tray (a cat litter tray works well)
> 2 one-pound coffee cans, filled with sand or stones
> 2 sticks, 24 inches long and 1 inch wide, or 2 yardsticks
> 8 to 10 thick rubber bands
> 1 piece of coat-hanger wire, or any stiff wire, approximately 18 inches long
> 1 ball-point pen tube
> hacksaw
> 1 clothesline spreader
> several same-sized nails

FILL THE CAN WITH SAND OR ROCKS.

Step 1. Attach 1 stick vertically to the outside of each coffee can by wrapping 3 or 4 thick rubber bands tightly around the can and stick.

Step 2. Cut a ball-point pen tube in half using a hacksaw. Secure one half to each upright stick with a rubber band about 12 inches from the top of the can. Keep the plastic tubes parallel to the floor.

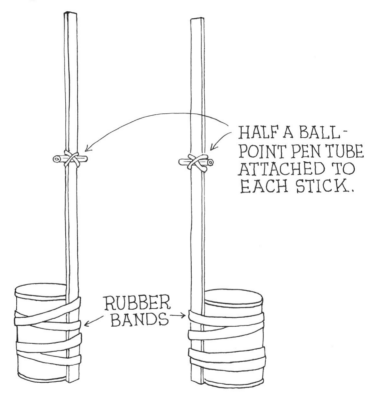

HALF A BALL-POINT PEN TUBE ATTACHED TO EACH STICK.

RUBBER BANDS

Step 3. Place the cans on either side of the tray. Slide the coat-hanger wire through the pen tube with the cup wheel and string collector, then through the pen tubes on the stand. Make sure the wheel is set high enough in the tray so that it doesn't scrape the bottom.

There are a few more things to do to get ready to experiment. Hang the clothesline spreader pulley from the top of a nearby ladder or chair. Thread the string from the string collector through the pulley, letting it hang to the floor. Finally, make some weights by wrapping nails together with a rubber band.

To make the wheel move, pour water from a container into the cups. (A half-gallon milk carton works well as a pourer.) The falling water will cause the cup wheel to rotate, and the string to wind up and lift the nail weights attached to it.

You can recycle the water by pouring it from the tray into a bucket. Since pouring water back and forth like this can be quite messy, try to do this activity in a bathtub, large sink, or outdoors.

You may have to do some trouble-shooting. If the cups scrape the side or bottom of the tray, adjust the height of the ball-point pen tubes on the stand. If the string keeps slipping off the pulley, make sure the string collector is in a straight line with the pulley. Check this by turning the wheel slowly and watching how the string travels through the pulley.

You are now ready to perform a variety of experiments to find out how much water is needed to lift a given amount of weight.

EXPERIMENTS TO TRY

- How much water does it take to lift two nails from the floor to the pulley?
- What happens when you pour the water quickly? Slowly?
- How much water does it take to lift three, four, five, and six nails? What is the maximum number of nails that can be lifted?
- Using the two-pulley arrangement from page 20, how many more nails can you lift?

Try making wheels with different-size cups and different-size plates. Using the same pouring speed as before, raise the nails to the height of the pulley. In this way, you will be able to compare how well the different types of wheels perform the same amount of work.

- What happens if you use 6-ounce cups instead of 3-ounce cups for the waterwheel?
- What happens if you use pizza plates with the 3-ounce cups?

• What happens if you change both the diameter of the wheel *and* the size of the cups?

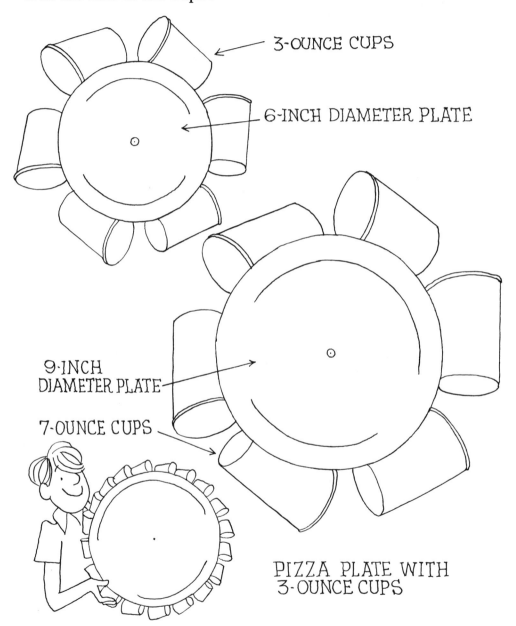

3-OUNCE CUPS

6-INCH DIAMETER PLATE

9-INCH DIAMETER PLATE

7-OUNCE CUPS

PIZZA PLATE WITH 3-OUNCE CUPS

FURTHER CHALLENGES

Now try directing the force of the water onto different parts of the wheel to see what effect this has on the power of your model. You will need a bucket filled with water and a garden hose or tubing of a similar diameter.

Put one end of the tubing into the bucket of water. Start the water flowing onto the wheel by sucking on the end of the tubing. While you are doing this and whenever you are applying water to the wheel, make sure this end is lower than the level of the water in the bucket. Your siphon arrangement should look something like this.

- Pour the water into the cups at the top of the wheel until the nails reach the pulley.
- This time place the end of the tubing so that the water goes into the cups in the middle of the wheel.
- Now try to lift the nails by siphoning the water into the bottom cups.

WHAT'S HAPPENING?

In the first group of experiments, you should have found that pouring water quickly or slowly will lift small numbers of nails. However, if you pour very slowly—just enough to keep the wheel moving—a smaller amount of water is used up than would be used if you pour quickly.

As you increase the number of nails, more water is needed to lift them. Finally, a point is reached where no matter how much water you pour on the wheel, it cannot lift a larger number of nails.

The water wheel is acting in a manner similar to the windlass. The weight of the water falling into the cups acts as a force to turn the axle, which is also the pivot point or fulcrum.

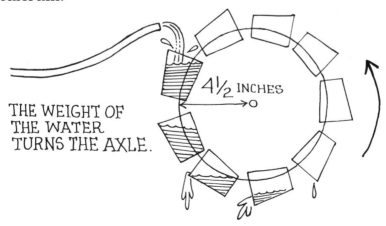

THE WEIGHT OF THE WATER TURNS THE AXLE.

4½ INCHES

To lift a small number of nails, the force needed to turn the axle is also small, and only a small amount of water is needed. The larger the number of nails, the more force is needed to turn the axle and lift the weights. Finally, if the weight becomes too heavy, even when each cup is filled with water, not enough force is exerted to turn the axle.

By using a pizza plate, as you did in the second set of experiments, you increase the distance from the fulcrum at which the force is exerted. By using 6-ounce cups, you increase the weight of the water. Increasing the diameter of the wheel and the force applied to it gives you greater leverage and enables you to lift heavier weights.

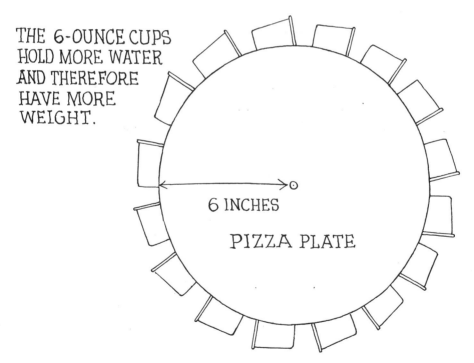

THE 6-OUNCE CUPS HOLD MORE WATER AND THEREFORE HAVE MORE WEIGHT.

6 INCHES

PIZZA PLATE

THE PIZZA PLATE HAS A LONGER DISTANCE FROM THE AXLE AND THEREFORE EXERTS A GREATER FORCE.

If you want to compare water wheels to determine which one is the most effective, it is useful to think about the amount of work each one can do. *Work,* in this situation, is defined as moving the same weight—the same number of nails—over the same distance, from the floor to the pulley.

There is one other important consideration. It will take a different amount of time for different-diameter wheels or ones with different size cups to lift the same weight. Compare the time it took each of your models to do the same work. The *power* of a machine is the amount of work done compared to the amount of time it takes to do it. The wheel that moves the greatest number of nails in the shortest amount of time has the most power.

The point at which the water hits the wheel is also important to the wheel's ability to do work. From the third set of experiments, you should have found that water pouring into the top cups lifted the wheel the fastest. You may not have been able to get the wheel to move at all when the water was hitting the bottom cups. This is because the weight of the water falling at the top pushes on the wheel for a greater distance than water hitting halfway down or at the bottom.

For a long time water wheels sat in streams or rivers. Their paddles or buckets were moved from the bottom by the flowing water. Gradually, people discovered that more power could be obtained by having the water fall on the top of the wheel.

Each type of water wheel was given a special name. In an *undershot* water wheel, the force of the water hits the bottom of the paddle.

In an *overshot* water wheel, the water falls into buckets on the top of the wheel.

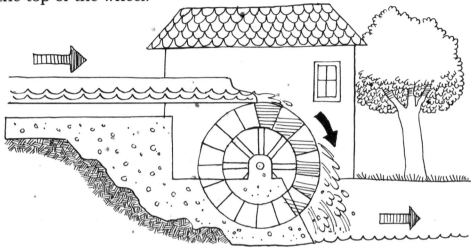

In a *breast* water wheel, the water falls on the side of the wheel into the buckets.

As you saw with your model, the overshot wheel makes the best use of the falling water. It is more powerful than the other two types.

MAKING A HORIZONTAL WATER WHEEL

When you turn on a light to read this page, the electricity that comes into your home or classroom has most likely been produced by a kind of horizontal water wheel called a *turbine.* You discovered through experimentation with your model that it made a difference where and how water was poured onto the wheel. Similarly, people in sixteenth-century Europe discovered that changing the wheel's position from vertical to horizontal made the water wheel a more powerful machine.

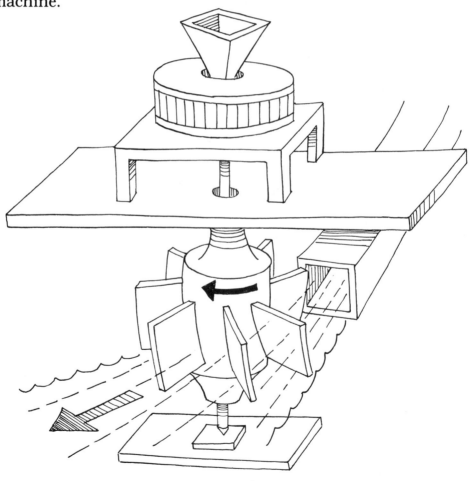

People continued to experiment, and many different kinds of wheels were built, especially in France and America. Each wheel was an attempt to improve upon past designs. This process eventually resulted in the development of the modern turbine, which is still used today to generate electricity.

One approach to improving water wheels was to make them smaller and have them move very fast. You, too, can take up the challenge of improving your water wheel by building a smaller, faster, horizontal model.

The water wheel used in the preceding sections can be used for some of the upcoming experiments, but you might have difficulty finding a tray wide enough to hold this wheel horizontally. Here is a way of making another smaller wheel following the same general procedure as before.

You will need:
        4 plastic plates, 6 inches in diameter
        1 plastic soup bowl, 6 inches in diameter
        12 plastic cups (3-ounce size)
        1 piece of wood, 3 inches wide and 6 inches long
        1 cat litter tray
        1 piece of coat-hanger wire or any stiff wire,
           approximately 16 inches long
      masking tape, 2 inches wide
      hammer
      1 nail
      scissors
      1 piece of ball-point pen tube

Step 1. Find the center of the plates and the soup bowl. (See page 52.) Punch a hole with a nail just big enough so that the coat-hanger wire fits through easily.

Step 2. Tape 2 plates and the bowl together on the wire as shown.

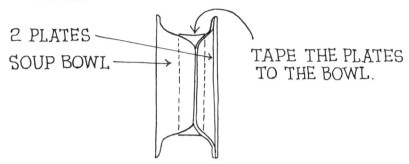

2 PLATES

SOUP BOWL

TAPE THE PLATES TO THE BOWL.

Step 3. Cut 6 plastic cups in half. Place 6 whole cups on the 2-inch-wide piece of masking tape according to the directions on pages 53–54. The 6 cups should be placed right next to each other.

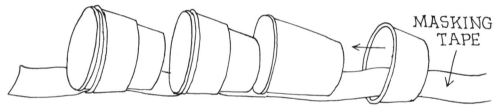

MASKING TAPE

THE CUPS ARE PLACED RIGHT NEXT TO EACH OTHER.

Step 4. Wrap the tape with the cups around the wheel between the bowl and plate and secure it in place with more tape.

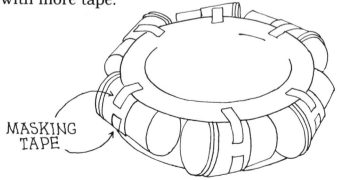

MASKING TAPE

Step 5. Hammer a hole through the center of a piece of wood with a nail. Then remove the nail. Make the hole big enough so that the coat-hanger wire will pass through it.

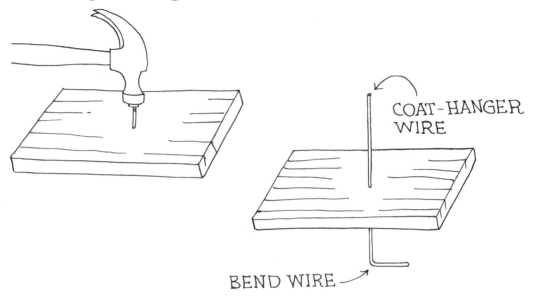

COAT-HANGER WIRE

BEND WIRE

Step 6. Push the wire through the wood. Bend a small portion of the wire and tape this end to the underside of the wood.

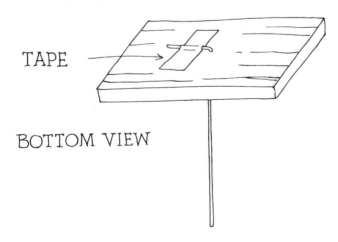

TAPE

BOTTOM VIEW

Step 7. Slide the piece of ball-point pen tube and then the assembled wheel onto the wire until the bottom of the pen tube rests on top of the wood.

COAT-HANGER WIRE

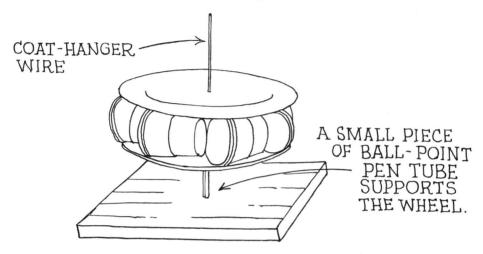

A SMALL PIECE OF BALL-POINT PEN TUBE SUPPORTS THE WHEEL.

Step 8. Make a string collector according to the directions on page 55. Slide it onto the wire and tape it to the water wheel device. Place this arrangement in the cat litter tray.

STRING COLLECTOR

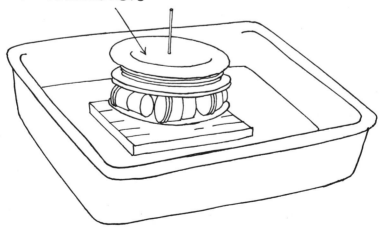

Making a Speed-Measuring Device

You will also need a way of measuring the speed of the wheel. Here is a simple device that will help you to do this.

You will need:

        1 block of wood, 3½ inches wide and 7 inches long

        2 blocks of wood, 3½ inches wide and 3½ inches long

        1 piece of coat-hanger wire or any stiff wire, 8 inches long

        1 piece of coat-hanger wire or any stiff wire, 10 inches long

        1 plastic juice container (12-ounce size) with lid

        60 feet of string

        hammer

        6 small nails

Step 1. Nail the 3 blocks of wood together so that the juice can will fit easily between the two vertical blocks.

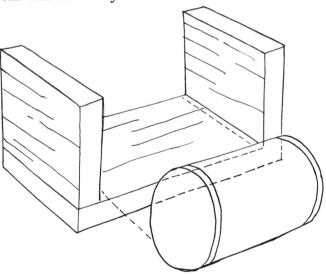

Step 2. Bend the 8-inch piece of wire in the middle to make a small loop. Nail or tape the ends of this wire to the sides of the two vertical supports.

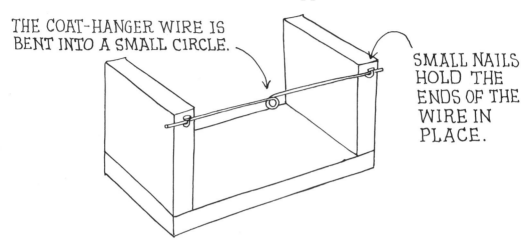

THE COAT-HANGER WIRE IS BENT INTO A SMALL CIRCLE.

SMALL NAILS HOLD THE ENDS OF THE WIRE IN PLACE.

Step 3. Carefully punch a hole through the center of the lid and the bottom of the juice can. (Look for the dot in the center of the lid or see page 52.) Place the 10-inch piece of coat-hanger wire through the holes. The holes should be big enough to allow the container to rotate freely on the wire axle.

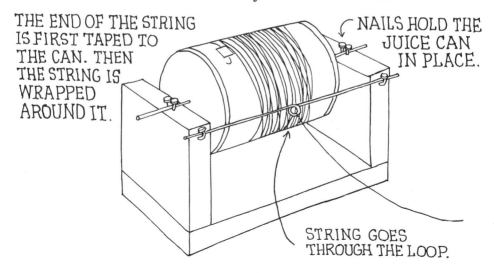

THE END OF THE STRING IS FIRST TAPED TO THE CAN. THEN THE STRING IS WRAPPED AROUND IT.

NAILS HOLD THE JUICE CAN IN PLACE.

STRING GOES THROUGH THE LOOP.

Step 4. Position the container and wire axle on top of the two wood-block supports. Hammer 2 nails into the wood on either side of the wire ends so that the axle can rotate but not slide around.

Step 5. Slip one end of the string through the wire loop and tape it to the container. Roll it up.

SETTING UP

Place the tray with your model turbine next to the speed-measuring device on the floor. Take a piece of coat-hanger wire about 8 inches long and make a small loop about ½ inch in diameter at one end. Tape this looped wire vertically to the side of the tray. Thread the end of the string from the speed-measuring device through the loop and tape it to the string collector on top of the wheel.

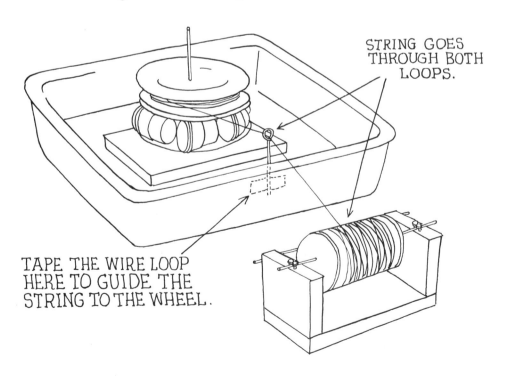

STRING GOES THROUGH BOTH LOOPS.

TAPE THE WIRE LOOP HERE TO GUIDE THE STRING TO THE WHEEL.

To operate your model, you will need to make a siphon as shown below. Before starting the experiments, make a trial run first. Direct the stream of water into the cups of the wheel and keep squirting water until all the string is wound up. Then pour the water from the tray back into the bucket and rewind the string on the speed-measuring device. If everything worked smoothly, you can begin experimenting.

EXPERIMENTS TO TRY

Play around with the tubing, trying different ways of squirting the water into the cups. Using the second hand of a clock, time how long it takes to use up all the string. Do this each time you change your technique. Keep a notebook handy for writing down your results the way scientists do.

- How long does it take to wind up all the string onto the string collector when the bucket is on a table and the wheel is on the floor?
- Place the bucket on a chair that sits on the table. If you squirt the water the same way, will it take a longer or shorter time to roll up the same amount of string?
- What will happen if the bucket is lower than the tabletop? Place the bucket on a chair. Do you think it will take a longer or shorter time to collect all the string?
- What happens when you squeeze the end of the tubing where the water comes out?
- Keeping the bucket at the same level, try a different diameter tubing. What happens if a smaller diameter tube—a tube from a ball-point pen, for example—is taped to fit snugly into the hose end? Will the wheel go faster or slower?

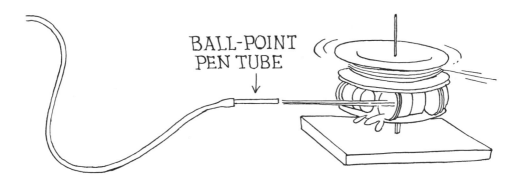

BALL-POINT
PEN TUBE

FURTHER CHALLENGES

- Make other wheels using different size or shape cups and see what happens. Here are some examples.

WHAT'S HAPPENING?

If you have done the timing carefully, you should find that the speed at which the horizontal water wheel turns depends on a number of things. Placing the bucket of water at a higher level will make the wheel move faster, while lowering the bucket will slow the wheel down. Squeezing the end of the tubing also will increase the speed of the wheel. Why?

The higher the bucket is, the longer the column of water inside the tubing. The greater the distance in height between the water in the bucket and the end of the tubing is, the greater the pressure where the water comes out. If you have several columns of water, each of a different height, the longest column would have the greatest amount of force at the bottom of it. And the greater the force at the bottom of the tubing is, the faster the water will come out.

Squeezing the end of the tubing also increases the momentum of the water. This momentum is a combination of the weight and speed of the water that keeps the water

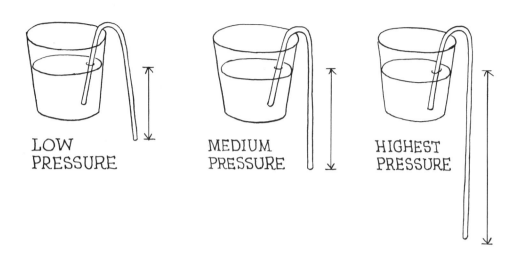

LOW
PRESSURE

MEDIUM
PRESSURE

HIGHEST
PRESSURE

moving. The water at the end of the tubing is being pushed out of the tube by the force of the other water behind it. This force remains the same no matter how you change the opening at the end of the tube.

Water cannot be squeezed together the way air can. Squeezing the end of the tubing doesn't squeeze the water. It just forces the water to move faster. This is similar to a large crowd pushing to get out of a building with two different size doors. Assuming that the people in the back are always pushing with the same force, the people exiting from a narrow door will have to move faster than those leaving through a wider door. The water leaving the tubing when you have narrowed the opening will have a higher speed and therefore a greater momentum. The greater the momentum of the water hitting the wheel, the faster the wheel moves.

However, if the opening becomes very small, it will let a much smaller quantity of water through each second—much smaller each second than with the wider openings. This water may be going at high speed, but because the quantity of water is much smaller, there is a decrease of overall momentum. Less momentum results in slowing down the wheel.

MAKING WATER WHEEL CONTRAPTIONS

The following contraptions demonstrate two systems of making machines move that are similar to arrangements made by people in the past. They are fun to make and operate.

A Mechanical Music Maker

This device is a primitive music machine. As the water wheel turns, it causes sticks to hit against glass bottles, making a clanking noise. Different rhythms can be created by moving certain parts on the drum of the machine.

You will need:

> vertical water wheel model (see pages 52–55 for directions on making one)
>
> 1 tray, at least 12 by 18 inches (a cat litter tray works well)
>
> 1 dowel, 36 inches long and ¼ inch in diameter
>
> 2 one-pound coffee cans with plastic lids
>
> 2 Styrofoam thread spools (1¼-inch size), or 2 rubber bands
>
> 2 or 3 plastic drinking straws
>
> 1 piece of coat-hanger wire or any stiff wire, approximately 24 inches long
>
> 5 half-gallon paper milk cartons
>
> 3 flat sticks, 1 inch wide and 1 foot long
>
> 3 empty glass jars (such as mayonnaise jars) or bottles, all the same size
>
> 1 piece of plastic tubing or garden hose, 4 feet long
>
> bucket

masking tape
hammer
1 nail

Step 1. Tape 2 milk cartons together lengthwise. Punch a
hole with a nail through the top corners on each
side of one of the cartons. Make sure both holes are
in the same position on each side. Repeat with 2
more milk cartons.

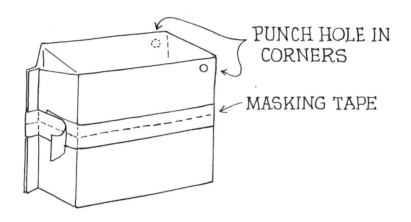

PUNCH HOLE IN
CORNERS

MASKING TAPE

Step 2. Place the plastic lids over the bottoms of the coffee
cans. Locate the small raised dot in the middle of
the lid. Punch a hole with a nail through this dot
and the bottom of the can. Do this for both cans.
With a pointed stick or pencil, enlarge these holes so
that the ¼-inch dowel will slide through easily.

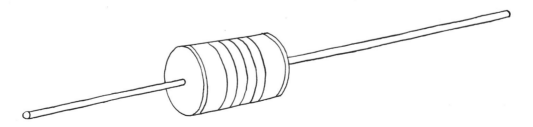

Step 3. Slide the 2 cans onto the dowel. Tape them together and secure them in place with Styrofoam spools or rubber bands on either side of the cans. (You may have to force the spool onto the dowel, but try not to make the hole too large or the tin-can cylinder won't stay in place.)

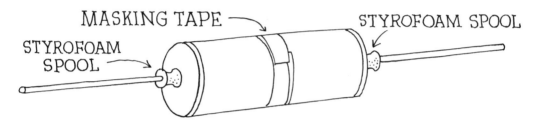

MASKING TAPE

STYROFOAM SPOOL

STYROFOAM SPOOL

Step 4. Slide the two ends of the dowel through the corner holes in the milk cartons so that one end of the dowel sticks out at least 12 inches. Slide the water wheel onto the extended part of the dowel, making sure it fits snugly. If the hole in the wheel is too big, you may have to put a Styrofoam spool on each side of the wheel. Test this arrangement to see if it's working correctly. If you turn the wheel with your hand, the tin-can cylinder should turn also.

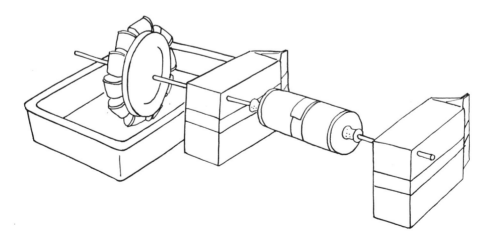

Step 5. Cut 3 strips from another milk carton, each
approximately 7 inches long and 1½ inches wide.
Fold them into triangular points, 1 to 1½ inches
high as shown.

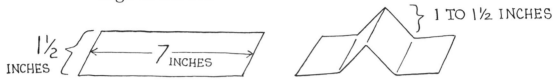

Tape these strips onto the coffee cans so that they
stick out from the cans. The triangular points
should be spaced about 3 inches apart. The points
should also be staggered—they should not be lined
up in one row across.

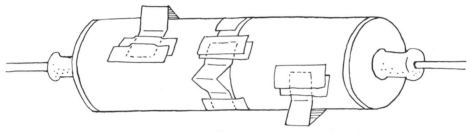

THE TRIANGLES STICK UP ON THE CAN. STAGGER THEM ON THE CAN.

Step 6. Cut the plastic drinking straws into 5 2-inch
segments. Slide them onto the coat-hanger wire.
Tape the ends of the wire securely to the top edges
of the 2 milk-carton supports.

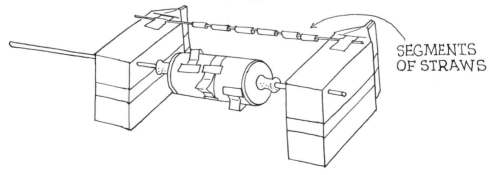

SEGMENTS
OF STRAWS

Step 7. Line up 3 jars in front of the coffee-can cylinder. Place the 3 flat sticks so that one end rests on top of a jar and the other end is an inch or so from the coffee-can cylinder. Tape the sticks to the first, third, and fifth pieces of straw.

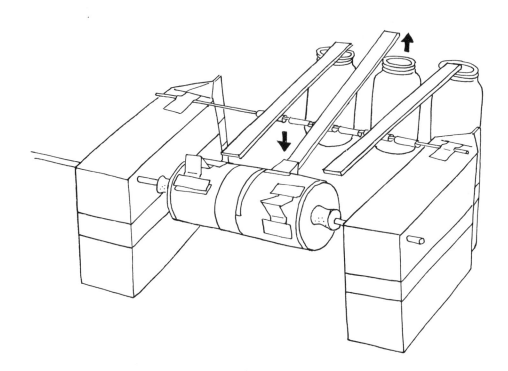

The sticks are now positioned so that as the coffee-can cylinder turns, the cardboard triangles make the sticks rise and fall. The placement of the sticks is important. Slowly turn the wheel by hand and watch how the triangles strike the sticks. If a stick is too far from a point, adjust and retape it.

Set up your siphon equipment to run the water wheel. The final arrangement should look like this.

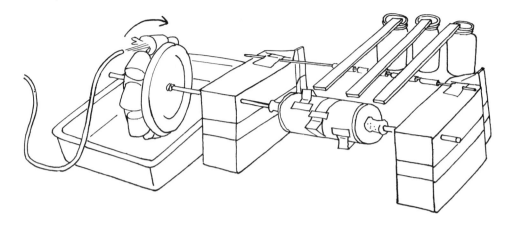

Siphon the water onto the wheel, making it move continuously. If all your adjustments are correct, each of the sticks will hit a bottle or jar, making a clinking sound. By placing the cardboard triangles in different positions on the cylinder, different rhythmic patterns can be produced. Try experimenting with other kinds of containers for the sticks to hit, or fill the bottles with water to different levels. How does the sound change?

The device you have just made is a kind of toy, but a similar arrangement was used by blacksmiths in water mills a long time ago. Heavy hammers were tripped by the turning shaft of a moving water wheel.

A Bubble-Blowing Device

Why wear your lungs out blowing bubbles when you can build a machine to do all the work for you? Here is a device that is fun to construct and observe in action. It uses the water wheel as a power source and a fan to blow bubbles continuously.

You will need:

> vertical water wheel model (see pages 52–55 for directions on making one)
> 8 half-gallon paper milk cartons
> 2 dowels, 36 inches long and ¼ inch in diameter
> 1 plastic box, at least 11 inches long (a shoe storage box works well)
> 1 cat litter tray
> 12 plastic plates, 6 inches in diameter
> 4 pipe cleaners
> ribbon, 6 feet long
> masking tape
> 1 piece of coat-hanger wire or any sturdy wire, 22 inches long
> 1 nail
> electric fan
> dishwashing soap

Step 1. Find the center of each of the plastic plates (see page 52) and make a hole large enough so that the ¼ inch dowel will slide through snugly. Tape together 6 pairs of plates as shown.

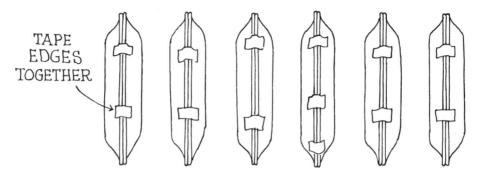

TAPE
EDGES
TOGETHER

Step 2. Tape 2 pairs together around the inside edges to make a wheel. Repeat to make 2 more wheels. (It might be easier to do this if someone is helping you hold the plates or if they are on the dowel.)

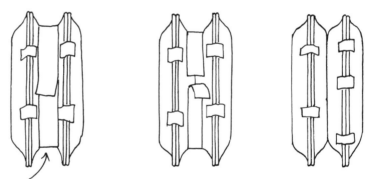

MASKING TAPE IS PLACED BETWEEN THE PLATES.

Step 3. Bend one end of a pipe cleaner to form a circle about 1 inch in diameter. Make 4 of these.

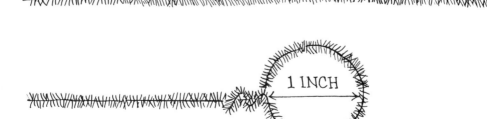

1 INCH

Step 4. Attach these 4 circles to 1 wheel as shown and tape securely in place. The pipe-cleaner circles should not stick out too far from the edges of the plate.

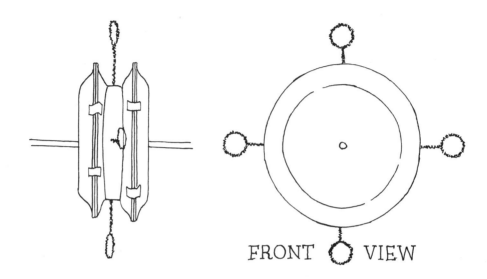

FRONT O VIEW

Step 5. Tape 2 milk cartons together as illustrated. Punch a hole with a nail through the top corners on each side of 1 of the cartons. Make sure both holes are in the same position. Repeat 3 more times.

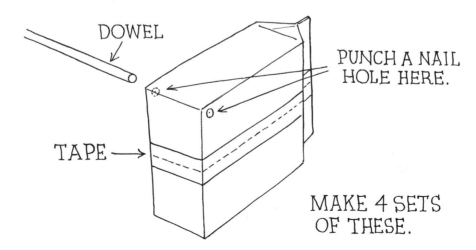

DOWEL

PUNCH A NAIL HOLE HERE.

TAPE →

MAKE 4 SETS OF THESE.

Step 6. Push the wheel with the pipe cleaners onto the dowel and place the dowel across the plastic box and through the milk cartons as shown.

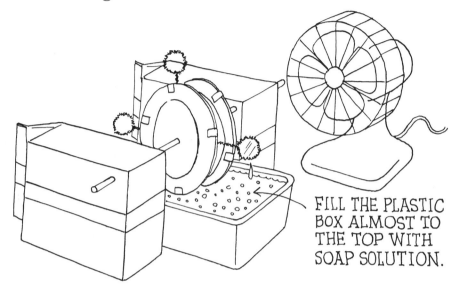

FILL THE PLASTIC BOX ALMOST TO THE TOP WITH SOAP SOLUTION.

Position this arrangement on a table in front of an electric fan.

Step 7. Fill the plastic box with soapy water nearly to the top. A good soap solution is 10 tablespoons of one of the more expensive dishwashing soaps to the amount of water in the box.

Step 8. Slide the water wheel onto the other dowel. Position the wheel above the center of the cat litter tray with the dowel. Push each side of the dowel through a milk carton for support. This arrangement should be on the floor beneath the bubble blower.

Step 9. Push a plastic-plate wheel onto the end of the dowel holding the bubble-blowing machine. Make a long continuous loop of ribbon around this plastic-plate wheel and the string collector on the water wheel.

Join the two ends of the ribbon together with masking tape. The ribbon loop should be adjusted so that it is neither too loose nor too taut. You will have to experiment until turning the water wheel results in easily turning the wheel with the wire loops.

The entire setup should look like this.

You may need to make some adjustments to get your bubble-blowing machine running smoothly. To check it out, turn on the fan and move the wheel with the pipe-cleaner wands slowly by hand. Each circle should dip into the soap solution and emerge from it with a soap film. The fast-moving air from the fan should then form the soap film into bubbles.

If this is not happening, first make sure the wands always emerge from the solution with soap film in their circles. Too many suds on top of the solution may be preventing this. Then try moving the fan closer or farther away from the plastic box or changing slightly the direction of the air coming from the fan. If the wheel slips while turning on the dowel, place a Styrofoam thread spool on each side of the wheel.

Before pouring water on the water wheel, test it by hand. Think of the two wheels with the ribbon connecting them as a pulley-and-belt system. As the water wheel turns, the plastic-plate wheel on the same dowel, or shaft, should turn also, making the ribbon move. The ribbon, in turn, moves the upper plastic-plate pulley wheel, causing the bubble-making machine to turn and the wands to dip into the soap solution. If your pulley wheels do not fit snugly on the dowels, secure them with Styrofoam spools.

Your apparatus should be ready to use. Turn on the fan, siphon or pour water onto the water wheel slowly, and watch as lots of bubbles blow across the room.

The pulley-and-belt arrangement used here is similar to those used in factories years ago. Some factories used to be a maze of leather belts turning all sizes of metal wheels. A leather strap ran from the shaft of the water wheel to a long shaft that held a bunch of smaller wheels. These in turn had smaller leather straps that operated the machinery. This was one reason water wheels were called prime movers.

THE WINDMILL

Have you ever opened a large umbrella on a windy day? The umbrella might turn inside out, or you could even be knocked over. Winds during a hurricane can reach 100 miles an hour or more, toppling huge trees. Even though air is invisible and doesn't weigh very much, it can still exert great force. Moving air, like flowing water, can also be used to generate power.

Windmills have not been around for as long a time as water wheels. It wasn't until after the tenth century that really practical windmills appeared. People in Holland and England used them the most because of the almost continuous winds that swept across areas of those two countries from the Atlantic Ocean. As with water wheels, the first windmills were used mainly to grind grain.

Eventually they also performed other kinds of work such as sawing wood. Windmills in operation today are used mostly to generate electricity or pump water.

Windmill shapes have changed a great deal since the first such devices were made in Persia in ancient times. These looked like large horizontal water wheels. Then for centuries windmills looked like very tall fans with four or six arms. Modern wind machines look more like airplane propellers with only two or three large, narrow blades.

Take one of your model water wheels and hold it up in front of you. Blow on it to make it move. Or bend over the horizontal water wheel and see if you can make it turn by blowing into the cups. Some modern water wheels may look like vertical windmills, and some horizontal windmills may look like water wheels, but windmill construction is different because of the different way air moves. Making model windmills and experimenting with them is a good way to find out about the motion of air around objects. The directions in this chapter will show you how to construct two types of windmills that were used for a long time in different parts of the world.

MAKING A HORIZONTAL WINDMILL

Horizontal windmills were used mostly in China, Persia (now known as Iran), and Iraq. Although improvements have been made in modern times, the same basic design is still being used in these countries today.

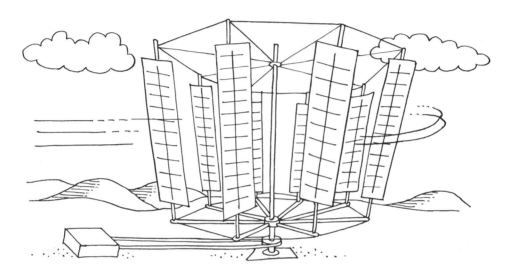

You will need:

    4 plastic plates, 9 inches in diameter
    1 piece of coat-hanger wire or any stiff wire, 16
        inches long
    1 half-gallon paper milk carton
    1 piece of ball-point pen tube, 3 inches long
    masking tape
    1 nail
    scissors

Step 1. Find the center of each plate (see page 52) and punch a hole just big enough for a coat-hanger wire to slide through easily.

Step 2. Tape 3 of the plates together as shown. Make sure the center holes are lined up with each other.

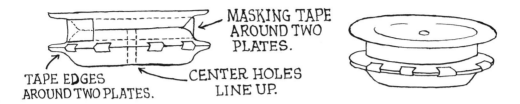

MASKING TAPE AROUND TWO PLATES.

TAPE EDGES AROUND TWO PLATES.

CENTER HOLES LINE UP.

Step 3. Cut each side of a milk carton so that you have 4 complete sides with triangular pieces at either end cut from the top and bottom parts of the carton.

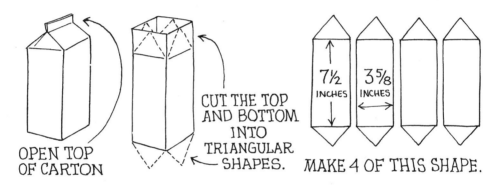

OPEN TOP OF CARTON

CUT THE TOP AND BOTTOM INTO TRIANGULAR SHAPES.

7½ INCHES

3⅝ INCHES

MAKE 4 OF THIS SHAPE.

Step 4. Place the piece of ball-point pen tube and then the wheel and string collector on the wire axle as shown.

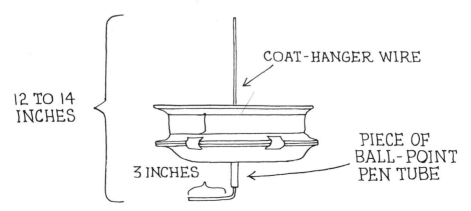

12 TO 14 INCHES

COAT-HANGER WIRE

3 INCHES

PIECE OF BALL-POINT PEN TUBE

Step 5. Tape the triangular flaps from one end of the 4 cardboard pieces to this set of plates.

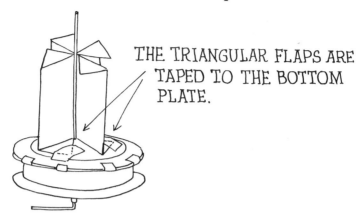

THE TRIANGULAR FLAPS ARE TAPED TO THE BOTTOM PLATE.

Then push the last plate onto the wire and tape the 4 top flaps to it.

This arrangement should look like a pinwheel.

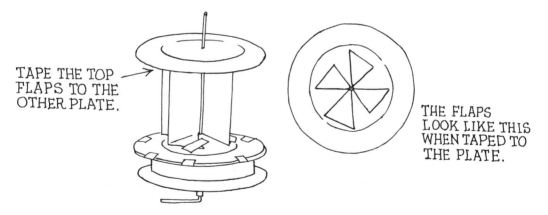

TAPE THE TOP FLAPS TO THE OTHER PLATE.

THE FLAPS LOOK LIKE THIS WHEN TAPED TO THE PLATE.

SETTING UP

You can use the coffee-can stand (see page 57), the speed-measuring device (see pages 73–75), and the string collector (see page 55) from the previous experiments with water wheels.

This version of the stand has two horizontal wires, each about 18 inches long. The top wire is held by the pen-tube pieces on the sticks and the bottom one is taped across the top of the coffee cans. Tape the wire axle to the middle of the lower wire. Attach the wire axle to the upper and lower wires with rubber bands. Tape the end of the looped-wire string threader to one of the sticks. Thread the string from the string collector to the windmill's string collector, and tape it to the windmill.

Your completed setup, with fan, should look like this.

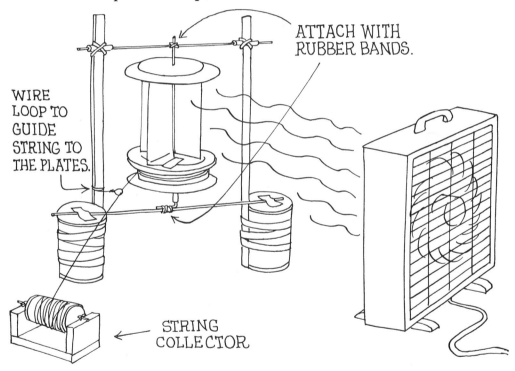

ATTACH WITH RUBBER BANDS.

WIRE LOOP TO GUIDE STRING TO THE PLATES.

STRING COLLECTOR

EXPERIMENTS TO TRY

Turn on the fan. Does your windmill move? If not, can you guess why? If you take a bird's-eye view of the situation, you can see what's wrong.

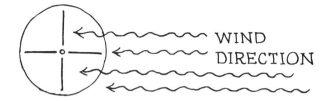

THE TWO ARMS CANCEL OUT EACH OTHER'S PUSHING ACTION.

WIND DIRECTION

Wind is pushing the cardboard on the left side. This should make the wheel move. However, the wind is also exerting the same force on the right side. The two forces, therefore, cancel each other out.

You can solve this problem by placing a shield on your windmill stand. To make a shield, cut a half-gallon milk carton in half and tape one side to one of the sticks on either side of the stand.

PLACING A SHIELD IN FRONT OF ONE HALF OF THE WINDMILL ALLOWS THE WIND TO MOVE ONE ARM AT A TIME.

WIND DIRECTION

When your shield is in place, only one arm at a time will feel the force of the wind. Each arm in turn will move the wheel as the wind strikes it. A real windmill of this type would require four shields because, unlike the breeze from the fan, wind changes direction.

Now that your model is in working order, try doing the following experiments:

• Using the speed-measuring device, see how much time it

takes to collect all the string when the fan is 6 inches from the model. Try again at distances of 1 and 2 feet. Keep moving the fan farther and farther away until the windmill will no longer turn.

- Set up your windmill model and fan on a table. Wrap all the string onto the windmill's string collector. Then take the other end of the string and pull it down over the edge of the table to the floor. Tie a very small nail to it. Place the fan close to the windmill and turn it on. If your windmill can lift this nail, try again with 2 and 3 nails.

- Double the size of the windmill blades by taping another piece cut from a half-gallon milk carton to each one. Repeat the experiments. Are you able to move the fan farther back now? Can you lift more nails?

WHAT'S HAPPENING?

The horizontal windmill does not move very fast; nor is it very powerful. In experimenting with your model, you should have discovered that it barely moves even when a fan is very close to the blades, and it lifts only a few nails.

The more surface area that is exposed to the moving air, the greater the force acting on that surface. The horizontal windmill has four blades or surfaces. However, because of the way they are situated, only one blade at a time is exposed to the wind.

In the next section you will see how to construct a model in which all four blades are continually exposed to the wind. The chief advantage of the horizontal windmill is that it will move no matter which way the wind blows.

MAKING A VERTICAL WINDMILL

You will need:

        1 tuna can (6½-ounce size)

        1 plastic soup bowl, 6 inches in diameter

        2 plastic plates, 6 inches in diameter

        2 pieces of coat-hanger wire or any sturdy wire, 16 inches long

        1 piece of coat-hanger wire or any stiff wire, 18 inches long

        1 half-gallon paper milk carton

        1 ball-point pen tube

        2 Styrofoam thread spools (1¼-inch size)

        masking tape

        hammer

        1 nail

        scissors

Step 1. Find the center of the tuna can, the soup bowl, and the 2 plates (see page 52). With a nail or other pointed object, carefully make a small hole in the center of each. This hole should be just large enough for a ball-point pen tube to fit through snugly.

Step 2. Make 4 very small holes through opposite sides of the soup bowl. These holes should be lined up so that the 2 16-inch pieces of coat-hanger wire will form a cross when pushed through the holes.

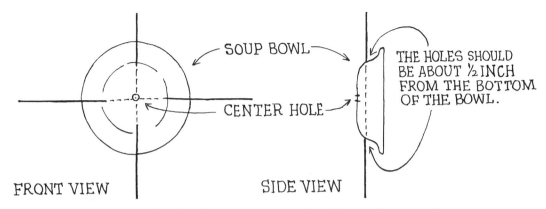

SOUP BOWL

CENTER HOLE

THE HOLES SHOULD BE ABOUT ½ INCH FROM THE BOTTOM OF THE BOWL.

FRONT VIEW

SIDE VIEW

Step 3. Slide the ball-point pen tube through one plastic plate, the tuna can, the other plastic plate, and the bowl with wire arms attached. Push a Styrofoam spool onto each end of the pen tube.

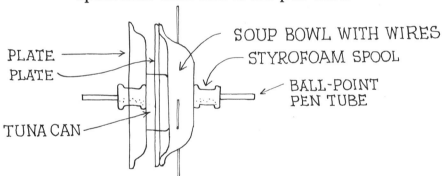

PLATE
PLATE

SOUP BOWL WITH WIRES
STYROFOAM SPOOL

BALL-POINT PEN TUBE

TUNA CAN

Step 4. Cut out 4 7½-by-3¾-inch pieces from the sides of the milk carton. Punch two very small holes in the middle of each piece about 2 inches from either end.

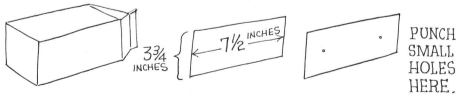

3¾ INCHES

7½ INCHES

PUNCH SMALL HOLES HERE.

Step 5. Slide these milk carton blades onto each of the wire arms of the soup bowl. One end of the cardboard blade can be taped to the soup bowl at an angle as shown. Make sure, though, that all the blades are slanted in the same direction.

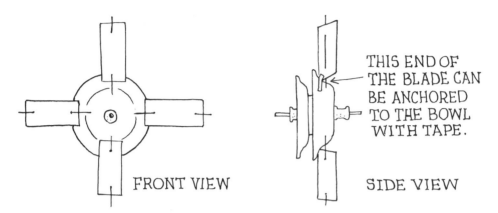

FRONT VIEW

THIS END OF
THE BLADE CAN
BE ANCHORED
TO THE BOWL
WITH TAPE.

SIDE VIEW

Step 6. Slide the 18-inch piece of coat-hanger wire through the pen tube in the center of the wheel.

SETTING UP

Once again you can use the coffee-can stand (page 57), the speed-measuring device (pages 73–75), and the fan from the previous experiments. Set up the vertical windmill as shown.

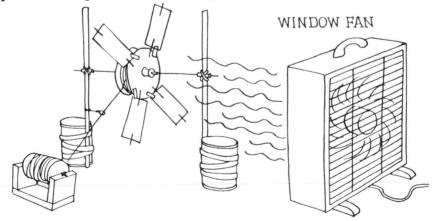

WINDOW FAN

To connect the speed-measuring device, tape one end of the string to the tuna can. Before you start, make sure you have a clock or watch with a second hand.

EXPERIMENTS TO TRY

- Change the angle of the blades in relation to the oncoming air from the fan. Here are three different positions.

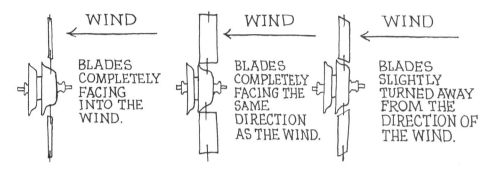

Using the speed-measuring device, time how long it takes to roll up all the string each time you change the angle of the blades.

- If you cut the cardboard blades in half, does the windmill travel faster or slower?
- Make a six-arm windmill by placing three pieces of coat-hanger wire into the soup bowl instead of two. Cut out more pieces of milk carton and insert them on the two new arms. Does the wheel go faster now?
- What happens as you move the fan farther and farther away from the windmill? What is the farthest the fan can be set back from the windmill and still make it move?
- What happens when the fan is placed at an angle from the windmill? Will it continue to move?

You can also try some experiments to see how much power your model can generate. Disconnect the speed-measuring device and tape a piece of string to the tuna can that reaches to the floor. Tie two same-size nails to the other end of the string.

- Turn the fan on and see if the windmill can lift the nails up to the tuna can. Keep adding nails until your model can no longer lift them.
- As you did before, try changing the angle of the arms, the size of the blades, and the number of arms. How do these changes affect the lifting power of the windmill?

WHAT'S HAPPENING?

You should have found that the larger the cardboard blades or the more arms used, the faster your model could go and the more nails it could lift. Why? Because the more surface area that is exposed to the wind, the greater the force exerted at the wire axle to do work. However, as the arms become larger, they also get heavier, and a point is reached where there isn't any gain in making them larger. Historically, people discovered the same thing. Windmills started out small, but eventually some in England and Holland had very large arms and a building several stories high to support them.

The angle at which the arms face into the wind also determines the amount of force the moving wheel will generate. For very large windmills, the most effective angle was found to be close to 15 degrees. Your model may give somewhat different results from this because of the simple materials and construction.

The vertical windmill is more powerful than the horizontal one. You can see why by comparing the amount of surface struck by the wind on the two different types. The wind is always moving against all four blades of the vertical windmill.

With the horizontal type, only one of the four surfaces is being pushed by the wind at any given moment.

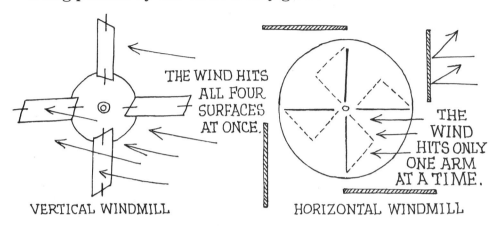

THE WIND HITS ALL FOUR SURFACES AT ONCE.

VERTICAL WINDMILL

THE WIND HITS ONLY ONE ARM AT A TIME.

HORIZONTAL WINDMILL

There is one big disadvantage to the vertical model, however. You may have discovered it while moving the fan around. The wheel will hardly move or may not move at all when the air is not blowing directly into it. To solve this problem, the people operating the large windmills had to rotate the top part of the mill to get the arms facing into the wind again. A long piece of wood attached to the top of the mill was used like a lever to move the arms around.

The miller also had to keep a close eye out for weather changes. If the wind speed became too fast, he either had to move the arms so they would no longer face directly into the wind, or turn on a brake. However, the brake could sometimes generate so much heat that a fire would start burning down the wooden mill.

The advantages of the less powerful horizontal windmill are that it is much easier to construct and when shields are in place, it will move in whatever direction the wind is blowing.

Using plastic cups and plates, and following the design of the vertical windmill, try to invent other kinds of windmills.

THE PADDLE WHEEL

Water wheels and windmills use the energy of flowing water and moving air to do work. We can also use the same wheel devices to move water and air. Can you think of some times when you would want to do this instead?

If you compare an electric fan to some of the vertical windmills, you will see a real similarity. Spin one of your models. Can you feel a slight breeze? Some fans used in factories or on top of office buildings are quite large. When operating they circulate large volumes of air through the building.

Wheels have also been used to move water. These wheels are mainly in the form of paddle wheels on the sides of boats. The first boat with a steam engine invented by Robert Fulton in 1809 used such an arrangement. As steam power was further developed, large boats traveling up and down the Mississippi and other rivers were moved by large paddle wheels on each side or at the rear of the boat.

MAKING A PADDLE-WHEEL BOAT

You don't need a steam engine to experiment with models of paddle-wheel boats. Ordinary rubber bands can be your source of power. Using the bathtub or a wading pool as your test tank, you can have lots of fun testing different boats—including your own designs!

You will need:

    2 half-gallon paper milk cartons
    2 sticks, 10 to 12 inches long by 1 inch wide
       (12-inch rulers will work well)
    package of rubber bands, assorted sizes
    scissors
    masking or duct tape

Step 1. Cut out 8 pieces of cardboard from a milk carton, 4 pieces approximately 3 by 4 inches, and 4 pieces 3 by 2 inches. Since a milk carton is wider than 3 inches, measure it before cutting.

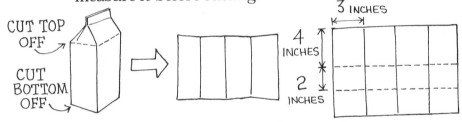

Step 2. Fold each piece in the middle to make a crease.

Step 3. Tape the 4 larger pieces together to make a cross. Then tape the 4 smaller pieces in the middle of each bend as shown.

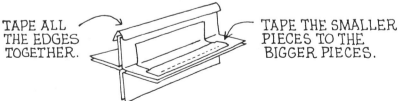

Step 4. Secure the 2 pieces of wood to the sides of the other milk carton with several rubber bands.

Step 5. Place a thick rubber band, about ¼ inch wide, on the ends of the two sticks. Slip the cardboard wheel in between this rubber band and twist it 10 to 15 revolutions, or until the band becomes very tight. Then let go of the wheel. The rubber band should untwist and spin the wheel.

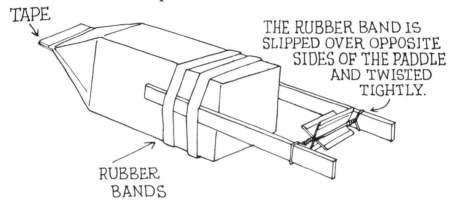

TAPE

THE RUBBER BAND IS SLIPPED OVER OPPOSITE SIDES OF THE PADDLE AND TWISTED TIGHTLY.

RUBBER BANDS

EXPERIMENTS TO TRY

Before you begin experimenting with your model, you should make a few test runs. Fill a bathtub or a wading pool with several inches of water. Place your boat in the water, checking to be sure that the wheel is not totally above the water or totally covered. You will have to keep trying until you find the best way for the boat to sit in the water. You can do this by changing the angle of the sticks on the sides of the milk carton.

To test your boat, wind up the wheel around the rubber band several times. Release the wheel and watch the action. Your boat should be propelled through the water.

One of the challenges of experimenting with this model is to see how long you can keep the boat moving. Try changing the different parts of the boat to see what happens:

- Change the size of the rubber band. Will a thicker rubber band enable the boat to travel longer?
- Will more rubber bands around the wheel make the boat travel longer?
- Will more arms on the wheel make any difference?
- Will a bigger paddle wheel make the boat move faster or travel farther?
- Double the size of the boat by placing another milk carton alongside the first and making a larger paddle. Will this make a difference?

WHAT'S HAPPENING?

Whether the boat moves or not and for how long depends on two major factors: the position of the wheel in the water, and the size and number of the rubber bands you use.

When you adjust the paddle wheel in the water, you are trying to match the force of the rubber band to the amount of water the wheel has to push against. If the paddles barely hit below the surface, there will not be enough water for the paddle to push against to move the boat. Since there is little resistance, the paddles will just splash the water.

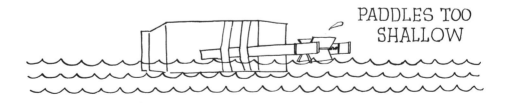

PADDLES TOO SHALLOW

If the paddles sit too deeply in the water, the boat won't move because the paddle does not have enough force to push against that much water. In one sense, the single paddle has to lift up water to keep moving. This additional force that is required is greater than the twisted rubber bands can deliver.

PADDLES TOO
DEEP

The best position for the arms of the paddle is where they dip a little way into the water. When the wheel turns, a small amount of water, neither too little nor too much, is pushed backward and the boat goes forward.

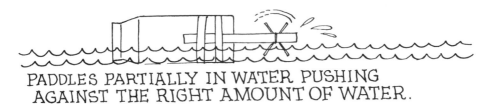

PADDLES PARTIALLY IN WATER PUSHING
AGAINST THE RIGHT AMOUNT OF WATER.

In designing a real boat, this type of problem can sometimes be figured out ahead of time by mathematical calculations. But tests on models still have to be carried out to arrive at the best possible position.

Rubber bands come in a variety of sizes and thicknesses. The size and thickness and the number of rubber bands you use will determine if your boat will move at all and how long it will keep moving. Twisting the paddle wheel around a thin rubber band and releasing it in the water probably will not move the boat. Using a thicker band or adding two or three more bands and twisting the paddle enough times will get the boat moving. However, if you keep adding more rubber bands or use very thick ones, a point will be reached where the paddle turns very quickly but the boat doesn't move. The power of the twisted rubber causes the paddles to splash lots of water, but this is not the same as their pushing against the water, and the boat cannot gain any momentum.

A similar situation happens with automobiles. If you start a car by giving the engine lots of gas and using a high gear, the rear wheels will spin and screech. The wheels are spinning so quickly that they are not gripping the road. The gasoline is wasted and the tires are worn away.

From these two examples you can see that it is very important to choose the right amount of power to operate a machine. By choosing the right size and number of rubber bands, you are matching the energy input with the energy need of your boat. Real paddle-wheel boats, cars, and other vehicles have gear systems (see pages 45–49) that enable the operator to match the speed of the engine with the speed of the wheels.

In the last set of experiments you increased the size of your paddle. You probably found that the bigger wheel increased the speed of your boat, but problems may have started to arise. If you make too big a paddle, the milk-carton boat tips over on its side easily. To prevent this tipping, you can place two milk cartons side by side with the larger paddle in between. This will make it more stable, but now you have added more weight and increased the surface in contact with the water. The larger the surface and the heavier the weight of the boat, the more power you need to move it. So, although you gained more power from a bigger paddle, its total increase is lessened by the need for a larger boat. As with the size of the rubber band, here, too, there has to be a balance between paddle size and boat size.

MODELS IN SCIENCE

As you have seen, models can be exciting to build and operate. They can be more than toys to play with because they present an opportunity to learn how machines function. Engineers often build small scale models to test out their designs. These models allow them to see what might go wrong and what parts might wear down quickly or break. Experimenting with models can also be a way of finding out how to make a machine more efficient. George Smeaton, an Englishman, built and tested several kinds of model water wheels. His arrangement was similar to the one used in this book. He demonstrated that overshot wheels made much more efficient use of flowing water than undershot wheels. Based on his experiments, most water mills after 1860 were of the overshot type.

Scientists also use models, but somewhat differently from engineers. Their task is to analyze a system or phenomena in order to understand what is happening. For instance, the movement of air around objects is very complex and still not fully understood. To gain some understanding of it scientists put simple objects in wind tunnels and use streams of smoke to see how air at various speeds moves around these objects. The results they obtain are useful in the design of airplanes, windmills, and tall buildings.

Try to use this technique yourself. When you want to get a good understanding of something, make a model of it. As you saw here, you can build all kinds of devices from such simple materials as plastic plates, cups, or tin cans. Using this approach, you may, in fact, come up with your own inventions.